Rob Webb and
Hal Westergaard

Insta... ..lle.ge ... cy

AS Sociology

Contents

Published by HarperCollins*Publishers* Ltd
77-85 Fulham Palace Road
London W6 8JB

First published 2002
This new format edition published 2004

ISBN 0 00 717270 2

British Library Cataloguing in Publication Data
A catalogue record for this book is available from the British Library.

Edited by Jenny Draine
Production by Katie Butler
Design by Gecko Ltd
Illustrations by Gecko Ltd
Cover design by Susi Martin-Taylor
Printed and bound by Printing Express Ltd, Hong Kong

Acknowledgements

The Author and Publishers are grateful to the following for permission to reproduce copyright material:

Alienation and Freedom by R. Blauner published by the University of Chicago Press, 1964 (graph on page 75)

Birmingham Department of Education, 1995 (bar chart on pages 45 and 52)

National Statistics: Social Inequalities published by The Stationery Office, 2000 (bar chart on page 14)

National Statistics: Social Trends published by The Stationery Office, 2001 (table on page 58)

Sociology: Themes and Perspectives by Haralambos and Holborn, Fifth Edition published by HarperCollinsPublishers Ltd, 2000 (table on page 41)

The Sociology of Work by K. Grint published by Polity Press, 1998 (graph on page 77)

Photographs

Kunsthistorisches Museum, Vienna 7

Every effort has been made to contact the holders of copyright material, but if any have been inadvertently overlooked, the Publishers will be pleased to make the necessary arrangements at the first opportunity

Get the most out of your Instant Revision pocket book

1 **Maximize your revision time.** You can carry this book around with you anywhere. This means you can spend any spare moments revising.

2 **Learn and remember what you need to know.** The book contains all the really important facts you need to know for your exam. All the information is set out clearly and concisely, making it easy for you to revise.

3 **Find out what you don't know.** The *Check yourself* questions help you to discover quickly and easily the topics you're good at and those you're not so good at.

What's in this book

1 The facts – just what you need to know

- The chapters in this book cover **all the AQA AS Sociology topics** as follows:
  - Chapters 1, 2 and 3 cover all three AQA Unit SCY1 topics: Families and households; Health; Mass media.
  - Chapters 4, 5 and 6 cover all three AQA Unit SCY2 topics: Education; Wealth, poverty and welfare; Work and leisure.
  - Chapter 7 covers the only AQA Unit SC3W topic: Sociological methods.
- This book also covers the following **OCR AS Sociology topics**:
  - Unit 2532, The individual and society, is covered in Chapter 8.
  - The Unit 2533 topic, Family, is covered in Chapter 1, and the Unit 2533 topic, Mass media, is covered in Chapter 3.
  - Unit 2534, Sociological research skills, is covered in Chapter 7.

- Most chapters are sub-divided into two clear **sub-sections**, which will help you to **organize your revision into manageable, short sessions**.

2 *Check yourself* questions – find out how much you know and improve your grade

- The questions are quick to answer. They are not actual exam questions. However, the authors, who are examiners, have written them in such a way that they will highlight any gaps in your knowledge and understanding.
- The answers are given at the back of the book. When you have answered the questions, check your answers with those given.
- There are marks for each question. If you score very low marks for a particular *Check yourself*, this shows that you are weak on those aspects of the topic and you need to put in more revision time there.

Revise actively!

- **Start your revision early.** Make a realistic revision timetable that allows for some relaxation time away from your books.
- **Concentrated, active revision** is much more successful than spending long periods reading through notes with half your mind on something else.
- For each of your revision sessions, choose no more than two topic sub-sections (half a chapter) and concentrate on reading and thinking them through for **20–25 minutes**. Then do the *Check yourself* questions. If you get a number of questions wrong, you will need to return to those aspects of the topic at a later date. Some Sociology topics are hard to grasp but, by coming back to them several times, your understanding will improve and you will become more confident about using them in the exam.
- Use this book to revise either on your own or with a friend!

Perspectives on the family

There are five perspectives on the family and its role in society:

- **Functionalists** believe that the family plays an important part in maintaining social stability by performing essential functions. **Murdock** argues that in all societies the family performs four basic functions: stable satisfaction of the sex drive, reproduction of the next generation, socialization of the young and satisfaction of economic needs. **Parsons** argues that the modern nuclear family performs two essential functions: **primary socialization** and the **stabilization of adult personalities**.
- **Feminism** argues that the family subordinates and **oppresses women**. Feminists divide into three main types:
  - **Radical feminists** argue that men benefit from women's oppression. They highlight the effects of **patriarchy**, a system of male power over women based on patriarchal ideology and the threat of violence.
  - **Marxist feminists** argue that women's oppression benefits capitalism. **Bruegel** argues that women's unpaid domestic labour helps to maintain capitalist exploitation by **reproducing the labour force** at no cost to the employer, by servicing the present generation of workers and by rearing the next generation of workers. Both radical and Marxist feminists argue that revolutionary change and the abolition of the family are needed to end women's oppression.
  - **Liberal feminists** argue that women's oppression can be gradually overcome by reforms (such as divorce, equal pay, etc.) and changing the attitudes and socialization patterns of both males and females. They believe that we are moving towards greater equality in the family.
- **Interactionism** focuses on the **meanings** people give to their own and other people's actions, including the way they construct and respond to family life. **Cooper** describes cases where individuals have withdrawn into mental illness rather than accept the narrow

conformity that their families demand. By contrast, **Berger and Kellner** see the family as an institution that offers scope for people to achieve fulfilment by creating the relationships they want.

- **New Right** thinkers believe that the 'traditional' patriarchal nuclear family – with a breadwinner-husband and homemaker-wife – is the kind best equipped to be self-reliant rather than depending on the welfare state. **Murray** argues that welfare provision has created a **dependency culture**. However, he has been strongly criticized, for example, by **Dean and Taylor-Gooby**.

- **Post-modernists** argue that the family no longer conforms to a single type. For example, **Stacey** believes that it no longer makes sense to see the nuclear family as the dominant family structure. Different kinds of household now co-exist. Family structure is in a **constant state of change** and families are fashioned and re-fashioned to meet changing needs.

  Giddens sees these changes as part of a **transformation of intimacy**, a move away from tradition, giving couples much more choice about personal relationships.

The family and industrialization

As society changes, so too does the family. What impact have economic changes like industrialization had on the family?

- Parsons argues that the nuclear family uniquely fits the needs of industrial society. In pre-industrial society, kinship dominates all aspects of life and the multi-functional **extended family** is the typical family structure.

  In industrial society, the smaller, more streamlined **nuclear family** unit is dominant. The nuclear family performs only two essential functions (see page 1). The nuclear family is **structurally isolated**: free from binding obligations to wider kin. This means that it can be **geographically** and **socially mobile**. Thus the nuclear family 'fits' industrial society, which needs a workforce able to move to where the work is and where status is based on individual achievement.

Social change brings about **structural differentiation**: institutions become more specialized in the functions they perform. Institutions like the state take on functions formerly performed by the extended family (e.g. education), leaving the nuclear family to specialize in its two essential functions.

Parsons' 'before and after' description of family structure has been brought into question by evidence from **Willmott and Young**, **Laslett**, **Anderson** and others.

- Willmott and Young identify three stages in the development of the British family:
  - **Stage One** (up to about 1750): the pre-industrial family was a unit of economic production and **nuclear families** were the main type.
  - **Stage Two** (from about 1750 to 1900): most working class families in industrial areas were **extended families** and there was an increasing separation between home and work.
  - **Stage Three** (from about 1900): improved standards of living mean there is now less dependence on the extended family and **symmetrical nuclear families** have increasingly become the norm.
- Laslett suggests that in **pre-industrial England, the nuclear family was the norm**. Using parish records, he shows that the average household size from 1564 to 1821 remained at 4.75 persons and most households comprised only two generations. However, such households may have had *family* ties with kin living nearby.
- Anderson uses **exchange theory** in his study of **extended family networks among industrial workers** in 19th century Preston. At a time of poverty and insecurity, the extended family provided assistance to those who were looking for work or accommodation when they arrived in Preston. Kin were used for childcare while parents went out to work. These relationships – being based on economic dependence – began to decline later in the 19th century as social conditions improved.

Check yourself

Families and households

Perspectives on the family

1 Read statements **A–E** about the family and identify the perspective associated with each one.

A 'If people are to be self-reliant, we must stick to a traditional clear-cut division of labour between husbands and wives.' (1)

B 'In today's society, there is no longer such a thing as "the family" – people now make their own choices and arrangements about what kind of set-up they want, so we get more and more diversity.' (1)

C 'The family performs an essential role in socializing the next generation into society's shared values.' (1)

D 'The family oppresses women, but through changing the way in which the next generation is socialized, we can gradually achieve equality between men and women in the family.' (1)

E 'To understand families, we have to take into account the meanings that family members give to situations.' (1)

2 According to Parsons, what are the two essential functions that the nuclear family performs? (2)

3 Explain what is meant by the term 'patriarchy'. (1)

4 Explain the differences between the radical feminist and Marxist feminist views of the family. (2)

The family and industrialization

1 What is meant by the 'structurally isolated nuclear family'? (1)

2 Explain the difference between geographical and social mobility. (2) Why might nuclear families promote geographical mobility? (1)

3 Identify Willmott and Young's three stages of family history. (3)

4 Why might the statistics that Laslett uses about households give a false picture about extended family ties? (1)

The answers are on page 107.

Roles and relationships within the family

Couples

Sociologists have examined the domestic division of labour, the distribution of resources in households, decision-making and domestic violence.

- **The division of labour** **Bott** distinguishes between **joint conjugal roles** – where husband and wife share tasks and activities – and **segregated conjugal roles**, where tasks and activities are separate and different. Is the traditional segregated pattern of breadwinner-husband and homemaker-wife being replaced by relationships based on equality and shared responsibility?

  Willmott and Young argue that it is, and that joint conjugal roles are more common among couples who are young, affluent and socially and geographically mobile. They see this as part of an overall trend towards a **symmetrical family**. Such couples share domestic tasks, wage-earning and leisure activities.

  Oakley criticizes Willmott and Young's conclusions and argues that they greatly exaggerate the extent of equality in marriage. Her **research on housework** shows that women shoulder most of the burden for housework and childcare and that men's contribution to domestic work is minimal.

  Since Oakley's research in the 1970s there has been a trend towards dual income families as a result of more married women going out to work. However, studies show that men's contribution to domestic work has changed very little. **Arber and Ginn** show that most women now carry a double burden of paid and unpaid work. **Irwin** concludes that women's improved position in paid work has made little difference at home.

  Silver and others describe a trend towards the **industrialization of housework** brought about by the expansion of service industries (e.g. food-processing, restaurants and childcare), and by the increases in women's employment and earnings. However, this may only apply to a minority of women who can afford such services.

Morgan suggests that these gender inequalities arise because **caring and emotional work** is central to the way **sexual difference** is defined in our society. **Dunne** confirms this in her research on lesbian couples. These couples viewed domestic work positively and were much more likely to share it equally than heterosexual couples.

- **The distribution of resources** This is ultimately a question of power and control. **Pahl** shows that men usually control financial resources, while women have the job of managing them. **Piachaud** shows that the distribution of resources in poor families can be highly unequal. Women often deprive themselves to maintain the standard of living of other family members.
- **Decision-making** **Edgell** found among professional couples that 'very important' and 'important' decisions were either made by husbands or jointly, whereas wives alone made the 'trivial' day-to-day decisions. He argues that differences in power to make decisions stem from differences in men's and women's earning power.
- **Domestic violence** **Dobash and Dobash** found that most domestic violence occurs within marriage. They suggest that this is because marriage confers power on husbands and dependency on wives. **Radical feminists** argue that violence or the threat of violence is a means by which men control women and perpetuate gender inequality.

Children and childhood

Historical and cross-cultural studies show that childhood is not a fixed biological stage, but **a social construct: a stage that is defined socially and culturally**. Being a child means different things in different societies. In some societies, childhood may not exist as a stage at all. Childhood is an **age-status** defined by various social boundaries and transitions. For example, in Britain laws define what a child can and cannot do, such as laws introduced in the 19th century making child labour illegal and schooling compulsory.

Aries draws a contrast between modern society, where childhood is a distinct stage, and medieval society, where there was little difference between children and adults. Paintings of the period show children as miniature adults, whereas by the 18th century, **a cult of childhood emerged**.

Postman argues that the mass media are bringing about **the disappearance of childhood**. In the 19th century, schooling and mass literacy created a sharp division between children and adults based on the ability to read. Today television breaks down the division between child and adult by making the same information available to everyone.

Gittins criticizes studies that treat childhood as if it were the same experience for all children. Such approaches fail to recognize the diversity of children's circumstances and the extent of inequality and power differences. By focusing on **diversity and inequality**, we can explain child abuse and exploitation.

Family diversity and changing family patterns

Changing patterns of marriage, cohabitation, divorce and childbearing, along with changes in social attitudes and behaviour, have created an increasing diversity of household types and living arrangements.

Nuclear families have decreased as a proportion of all households. An increasing proportion of households are now reconstituted or stepfamilies, lone-parent families or one-person households.

Family diversity

Rapoport and Rapoport identify five types of family diversity in modern Britain:

- **Organisational**: different patterns of domestic and paid work, e.g. male-breadwinner; dual-income or lone-parent families.
- **Cultural**: differences based on religion or ethnicity, e.g. Asian extended families; matrifocal Afro-Caribbean families.
- **Social class** differences: e.g. joint conjugal roles in middle-class couples, segregated ones in working-class couples.
- **Life stage**: different stages of the family cycle, e.g. newlyweds; couples with children; retired couples.
- **Cohort**: differences between generations, e.g. in attitudes to cohabitation and divorce.

The above helps to identify different types, but has been criticized for being too rigid and underestimating the extent of diversity. Morgan argues that there is now an almost infinite variety of families and households.

Perspectives on family diversity

There are broadly two ways of interpreting the trend towards diversity:

- The **New Right** and **functionalism** see the nuclear family as the 'correct' and 'normal' type of family structure. Other types of household are seen as incomplete or dysfunctional. The New Right see any trend away from the traditional patriarchal family as a change for the worse. Functionalists see a sexual division of labour between the male's **instrumental** (breadwinning) role and the female's **expressive** (nurturing) role as the most effective way of performing the family's essential functions. Thus these perspectives do not welcome increased diversity.

- Perspectives such as **radical feminism, interactionism and postmodernism** do not assume the nuclear family is the norm, but define families in a much more open-ended way. In this view, a family is any set of relationships defined as a family by the people involved. Sociologists using this definition would, for example, include **gay and lesbian households** in their definition of a family. **Weeks** describes such households as alternative families and gives them as an example of friendship and kinship.

Many changes to the family and marriage can be understood as part of what Giddens calls the **transformation of intimacy**. Couples now have more choice and what keeps them together is the quality of their personal relationship rather than economic dependence, obligations to the extended family or a sense of duty. This change affects not only divorce and remarriage, but also attitudes towards cohabitation and childbearing outside marriage.

Mitchell and Goody point to a decline in the stigma attached to divorce, cohabitation and births outside marriage and growing **tolerance of alternatives**.

Changing family patterns

- **Marriage and cohabitation**
  - Most adults are married and many re-marry after divorce.
  - Over the last thirty years, however, the age of first marriage has increased and the number of first marriages has fallen to an 80-year low.
  - Cohabitation has increased.

  These changes partly reflect the changing position of women and dissatisfaction with traditional marriage.

  Macklin identifies different types of cohabitation:
  - temporary casual convenient
  - affectionate dating
  - trial marriage
  - temporary alternative to marriage
  - permanent alternative to marriage.

- **Childbearing** In general, women are having fewer children, having them later or remaining childless. **Beck** suggests that these changes reflect a growing contradiction between women's domestic obligations and paid employment.

The proportion of births outside marriage has increased to about 40 per cent of all births, but this is mainly due to births to cohabiting couples rather than to single parents.

There is no longer the same stigma attached to births outside marriage and there is less emphasis on the importance of the family as an institution.

- **Divorce** There has been a rapid rise in divorce in Britain since the 1970s and about 40 per cent of all marriages end in divorce. There are several possible reasons:
  - **legal changes**: the 1969 Divorce Act widened the grounds for divorce to 'irretrievable breakdown', making it easier to obtain
  - **changes in women's position**: more job opportunities for women have made them less dependent on their husbands, as has the availability of welfare benefits
  - **secularization**: decline in the influence of religion
  - **less stigma** attached to divorce
  - **higher expectations**: people expect more from marriage and so become dissatisfied more easily.

Rising divorce rates are open to different interpretations. **New Right** thinkers argue that they signal a decline or even a crisis in the family caused by growing irresponsibility and permissiveness. **Functionalists** argue that divorce is not evidence of decline but a result of higher expectations and a trend towards equality between husbands and wives.

Hart, a **Marxist feminist**, argues that rising divorce rates reflect the conflicting demands of women's roles, at home where they are unpaid domestic workers and at work where they are a source of cheap labour.

The New Right and others assume that divorce always has negative effects on children, but **Bernardes** observes that divorce may be less damaging to children than a 'stable' marriage with constant conflict.

Mitchell and Goody identify a growing crisis of fatherhood where children lose contact with divorced fathers.

Divorce and remarriage add to the overall trend towards family diversity. Sociologists are interested in the way families are **reconstituted** after divorce and how relationships are maintained with ex-family members. One example is Stacey's research; another is **Smart**, who shows the key role that mothers play in maintaining relationships between children and their fathers after divorce.

Families and social policy

Family roles, relationships and structures are influenced by laws (e.g. divorce, abortion) and government policies on social security, taxation, health, education, etc.

Functionalists like **Fletcher** see social policy (such as welfare provision or divorce laws) as part of a '**march of progress**' towards a society where the family is given support by the state. This contrasts with the view that social policy is a form of social control by the state.

New Right thinkers believe that social policy should support the traditional nuclear family with a breadwinner-husband, homemaker-wife. This means encouraging **self-reliance**, e.g. encouraging fathers to provide for their dependants. They believe this would discourage the growth of a **culture of dependency**, which the New Right sees as a major cause of social problems. For example, generous welfare benefits discourage men from taking responsibility for their children, creating lone-parent families with no male role models, unruly and delinquent children, and a growing underclass. The New Right solution is policies to reduce benefits and encourage self-reliance.

Feminists argue that social policies work against women in areas such as housing, taxation and social security because they are based on the assumption that a wife and children are or should be dependent on a male breadwinner.

Donzelot sees the family as a channel though which the state and voluntary bodies regulate people's behaviour in areas such as sexuality, reproduction and education. He describes how social workers identify 'problem families' and place them under supervision and control. In these ways, the state controls the behaviour of the population through policies aimed at families.

Check yourself

Families and households

Roles and relationships within the family

1 Explain the difference between joint conjugal roles and segregated conjugal roles. (2)

2 What is a symmetrical family? (1) Suggest two factors which may have brought about its growth. (2)

3 Why does Oakley argue that the symmetrical family is a myth? (1)

4 Suggest three other aspects of husband-wife relationships apart from housework where there may be evidence of inequality. (3)

5 Explain what sociologists mean by the expression 'the social construction of childhood'. (1)

6 Suggest two factors that have helped to create childhood as a separate age-status in our society. (2)

Family diversity and changing family patterns

1 Name the five types of family diversity identified by Rapoport and Rapoport. (5)

2 Name one sociological perspective that would regard family diversity as undesirable. (1)

3 Approximately what percentage of (**a**) marriages end in divorce; (1) (**b**) births occur outside marriage? (1)

4 Identify two ways in which increased divorce might lead to increased family diversity. (2)

Families and social policy

1 From a New Right perspective, identify one of the ways in which generous welfare benefits can undermine the traditional family. (1)

2 Name one perspective or sociologist who sees social policy as a means of social control over families or individuals. (1)

The answers are on page 108.

Medical and social models of health

The **medical model** of health is based on knowledge about the physical and **biological causes** of disease. It sees health as the absence of disease. It developed with the growth of the medical profession and tends to take a **curative** approach. Doctors tend to favour this model.

Sociologists favour the **social model** of health, which focuses on the social distribution of health and illness between different groups (e.g. death rates vary between social classes). The social model is interested in the environmental and social causes of ill health. It tends to take a **preventative** approach. In recent years, doctors have begun to acknowledge the importance of social influences on health, such as stress factors and lifestyle, and it is now recognized that good health is more than merely an absence of disease. The World Health Organization defines it as 'a state of complete physical, mental and social wellbeing'.

Sociologists are interested both in how health and illness are **socially caused** and in how they are **socially constructed**. An example of the social causes of ill health is poor living conditions, while an example of the social construction of health is that different cultures have different ideas about what it means to be healthy or ill.

Sociologists use the term **illness** to describe the individual's subjective experience of 'feeling unwell'. The term **sickness** refers to a social status which is defined professionally, for instance, by a doctor who issues a sick note, while **disease** is a term to describe a biological malfunction.

Class inequalities in health and health care

'Health chances' refers to a person's chances of enjoying good health and long life (or suffering poor health and dying early). There are two main measures of health chances: **mortality** statistics (which measure death rates) and **morbidity** statistics (which measure rates of illness). Mortality statistics are more reliable than morbidity statistics because deaths can be counted more accurately than illnesses.

Studies provide evidence that health chances are unequally distributed. **The Black Report** (1980) showed that, despite the introduction of the NHS and an improvement in living standards over the previous 30 years, **a steep class gradient in health** remained. At all ages, lower social classes (measured by occupation) experience higher mortality rates for almost all causes of death. Recent evidence shows that the **health gap** between the classes has widened since 1980.

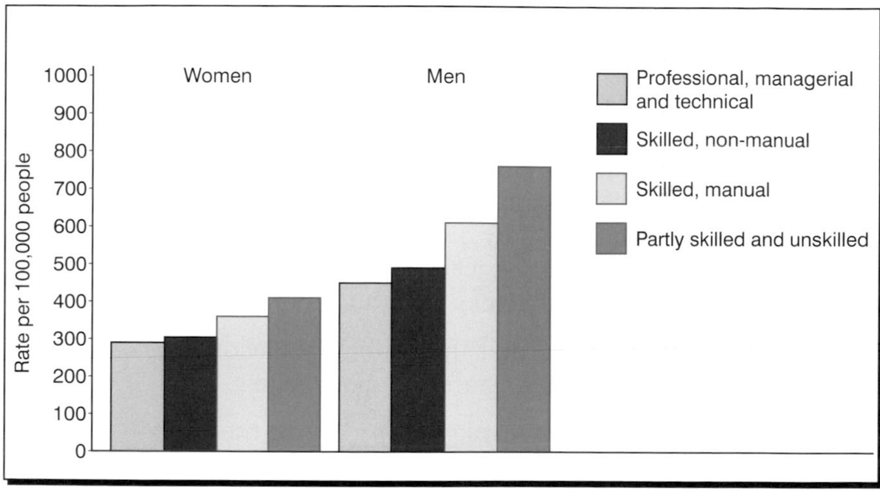

Age-standardized death rates per 100,000 people aged 35 to 64, England and Wales, 1986–92

The Black Report offers **four explanations** of class inequalities in health:

- **The social selection explanation** This is the view that illness is not the result of low income and poverty, but the **cause** of them. Healthy people are more likely to be upwardly mobile, while those who are ill become downwardly mobile, e.g. because they missed out on school through illness.
- **The artefact explanation** This view states that **statistical comparisons** between social classes tend to exaggerate the extent of inequality because the working class (the poor health class) is

shrinking while the middle class (the good health class) is expanding.

- **Cultural and behavioural explanations** Unequal health stems from differences in the behaviour of people from different classes: working class people have worse health because they are more likely to engage in **health-damaging behaviour**, such as smoking, drinking alcohol, etc. Some argue that behavioural differences between the classes result from **cultural differences**, however, **Marmot** shows that only a small part of the class gap in mortality is due to health-damaging behaviour.
- **Structural and material explanations** These see social inequality and material conditions as the cause of health inequalities. These include **poverty and material deprivation** stemming from unemployment, low income, bad housing conditions, polluted environments, and unhealthy or dangerous working conditions. Low social position is associated with a lack of control over one's life and with higher levels of **stress** and thus poor health.

The Black Report suggested that the cultural/behavioural and structural/material explanations are the most valid.

Graham argues that cultural explanations 'blame the victim' and that people engage in health-damaging behaviour like smoking because of structural factors such as poverty. She found that women in poor households smoked as a way to cope with stress.

Statistics show that the working class suffer worse health than the middle class. Do they therefore make more or better use of health care than the middle class? According to **Tudor-Hart**, there is an '**inverse care law**': the groups with the worst health (such as the working class) get the least access to health care resources, and **the middle class benefit most from health services**.

Cartwright's studies of the **doctor-patient relationship** illustrate this. She shows that although the working class make more use of health services (e.g. they visit GPs more often), the middle class get more from the system. Middle class patients have longer consultations and ask for and get more information from doctors. They are also more likely to get a second opinion, be referred to a consultant, gain admission to specialist hospitals, and make use of preventative and screening services.

Similarly, **Le Grand** shows that although the working class have poorer health, they receive proportionally less from the health service than the middle class. He estimates that when need is taken into account, class I receives over 40 per cent more health care from the NHS than class V. This is because although the NHS is free of charge, it is more costly for lower income groups to use it.

Gender differences in health and health care

Women live longer than men but they report more illness. However, because they live longer than men, women are more likely to suffer from chronic diseases. This partly explains why two-thirds of the disabled population are women.

There are **four main explanations** of gender differences in health and health care:

- **Biological** Cross-cultural evidence indicates that gender differences in mortality are largely biological in origin: women live longer than men in most societies. However, social factors do influence mortality rates. For example, women's life expectancy improved more than men's during the 20th century because of a dramatic decline in deaths in childbirth.
- **Artefact** In this view, higher morbidity rates for women could simply reflect a greater willingness or opportunity to seek help when they have symptoms of illness, and not greater sickness.
- **Cultural** There are two views about the influence of culture: the **'licence' view**, which suggests it is more acceptable for women to admit to being ill, and the **'women coping' view**, which suggests that women are expected to cope with being ill because of their domestic responsibilities.

- **Structural and material** Women spend more time at home, which means that bad housing is likely to affect them more. Women are also more likely to suffer poverty, e.g. as lone parents. **Bernard** shows that married women (and single men) have the worst health, including mental health, because married women sacrifice their own well-being for their husbands and families.

Most health care is provided by women:
- **Informal care** in the home, looking after sick children or elderly relatives, is generally seen as part of women's gender role.
- **Formal care** by paid workers is largely women's work too: most NHS employees are female.

Ethnic differences in health and health care

Some illnesses and conditions correlate with ethnic background. For example, those born on the Indian sub-continent have above average rates of heart disease, diabetes and tuberculosis but lower rates of cancer and bronchitis, while those born in Africa or the Caribbean have above average rates of stroke, high blood pressure and diabetes.

However, there are problems in comparing the health of different ethnic groups because ethnic categories are difficult to define, and because the health chances of an ethnic group tend to reflect its class position.

There are **three main explanations** of ethnic differences in health:

- **Genetic** There are links between certain **genetic disorders** and ethnic origin. For example, sickle cell disease is much more common among people of African ancestry. However, genetic differences between ethnic groups account for only a tiny proportion of all illnesses.

- **Cultural** These explanations focus on the **cultural norms, values and lifestyles** of ethnic groups. For example, heart disease among Asians has been blamed on the use of cooking fats. However, Nettleton criticizes explanations that blame minorities for health-damaging behaviour but overlook their healthy practices, such as low consumption of alcohol and tobacco, especially by Asian women.

- **Structural and material** Some ethnic minorities – notably Afro-Caribbeans, Pakistanis and Bangladeshis – experience high rates of unemployment, low pay, poor housing and limited educational opportunities. From this point of view, the poorer health of some ethnic groups is not caused by genetic or cultural factors but reflects their **class position** and the effects of **discrimination**.

Studies of the take-up of **health care** by ethnic minorities, such as **Rudat's**, suggest that problems of communication may result in minorities receiving poor quality care, including less effective consultations and below-average use of preventative services. Translation services are poor and health care staff are often unable to respond to the language needs of ethnic minority patients. Some argue that such barriers to access are a result of **institutional racism** in the NHS.

Check yourself

Health

Medical and social models of health

1 True or false?

A 'The medical model takes a preventative approach to disease.' (1)

B 'The social model is interested in the environmental causes of ill health.' (1)

Class inequalities in health and health care

1 Explain the difference between morbidity and mortality. (2)

2 Suggest two examples of aspects of health where there are class inequalities. (2)

3 Which explanation of class inequalities in health does each of these statements reflect?

A 'The working class are twice as likely to choose to smoke compared to the middle class, and this is why they have higher rates of illness.' (1)

B 'Working class people smoke more because they lead more stressful lives.' (1)

C 'Inequalities in health are not caused *by* class inequalities, they are the cause *of* these class inequalities.' (1)

D 'Factors like unemployment and poor housing are the main reason why working class people have worse health than middle class people.' (1)

4 Which explanations of class inequality in health are the following statements criticisms of?

A 'Good health doesn't in fact make much difference to a person's chance of being upwardly mobile.' (1)

Check yourself

B 'The ...... explanation of health inequalities is a 'victim-blaming' explanation.' (1)

5 What is the 'inverse care law'? (1)

Gender differences in health and health care

1 According to Bernard, which two of the following groups have the worst health: married men; married women; single men; single women? (2)

2 Identify two possible reasons why women have more consultations with doctors than men do. (2)

3 What is 'informal care'? (1) Why do women provide most of it? (1)

Ethnic differences in health and health care

1 Give one reason why it is difficult to compare the health of different ethnic groups. (1)

2 Suggest one reason why ethnic minorities do not always receive equal treatment in the NHS. (1)

The answers are on pages 109–10.

Medicine and the medical profession

Sociologists are interested in the impact and role of medicine and the medical profession in society. The general health of the population has clearly improved (e.g. during the 20th century, life expectancy almost doubled), but is this due to medicine and doctors?

Studies show that medical care and medical discoveries have often had relatively little influence on health compared with social factors.

McKeown's historical evidence suggests that medical care had relatively little effect on death rates before the 20th century. Most deaths were from infectious diseases (TB, cholera, measles, etc.), and the biggest improvements in health were brought about by **public health** measures such as improved sanitation, clean drinking water, and better **housing**, **diet** and a higher **standard of living**.

Illich goes further, arguing that modern high-tech curative medicine and the medical profession are a danger to our physical, mental and spiritual health. He uses the term **iatrogenic illnesses** – those caused by medical intervention – to describe this danger, such as the side effects of drugs, errors by doctors, etc. There has been a '**medicalisation of life**' and we have lost control over own bodies, lives, suffering and death and become dependent on the medical profession, the 'new priesthood'.

If medicine and the medical profession are not responsible for improvements in public health, what is their function? Different perspectives give different answers:

- **Functionalists** such as Parsons argue that being sick has potentially disruptive effects on society. **Sickness is a form of deviance** that needs to be controlled. Otherwise, the behaviour associated with it, such as dependency, apathy and incapacity, could become widespread and threaten the smooth functioning of society. It is therefore important to restrict access to **the sick role** to those who are genuinely sick. This is the function of the doctor, whose authority is maintained by his or her objective scientific knowledge and high status.

The sick role involves both **rights and obligations**: the right to be exempted from normal role obligations (such as work) and to be looked after, and the obligation to want to get better, to seek help and to obey doctor's orders.

Access to the sick role has to be legitimized by the medical profession. Failure to comply with its obligations may result in society withdrawing from the individual the right to be considered sick and/or imposing sanctions. The function of the medical profession is one of **social control**: it polices the sick role, ensuring that only the genuinely sick gain access to it.

Parsons recognizes that medicine and sickness have social as well as biological dimensions. However, he assumes that medicine is a 'good thing' and that the medical profession works for the interest of society. His explanation also fits short-term, curable illnesses better than long-term, chronic illnesses.

- **Conflict perspectives** include Weberian, Marxist and feminist approaches. They see the role of the medical profession differently. All of them see it as benefiting some special interest group rather than society as a whole.
  - **Weberians** such as **Freidson** see doctors as **self-serving** and using their monopoly of medical knowledge to preserve their own power and status.
  - For **Marxists**, medicine and the medical profession perform important **functions for capitalism**, but not for society as a whole. Doctors act as agents of **social control**, ensuring that an alienated workforce cannot escape to the sick role but remains at work to produce profits. They **reproduce the workforce** by 'patching up' sick workers. Ideologically, they **mask the exploitation** of capitalist society, making it appear more caring. Medicine and health care are also enormous **sources of profit** for giant multinational drugs companies.
  - **Feminists** see society as **patriarchal** and doctors as perpetuating this. Medicine has a **social control** function, ensuring that women are kept in a subordinate role, for example,

by controlling women's fertility (e.g. through the **medicalization of pregnancy and childbirth**, and control over access to abortion and contraception). **Doyal** describes how doctors often stereotype women as emotional, neurotic, less objective and more excitable than men. Even when there is clear evidence that a woman's problem is physical, doctors often see it as having a psychological cause.

The social construction of health, illness and disability

Health, illness and disability can all be seen as **socially defined or constructed**. That is, they are created by the labels, definitions or meanings that we attach to ourselves and others, and by the way we act upon these meanings. One example of social construction is mental illness, which is covered in the next section. Here we shall look at physical illness and disability.

Interactionists are interested in how individuals come to acquire **illness labels**, and the effects these labels have on them and those around them. They are interested in how **doctor-patient interactions** create such labels.

But how do people decide they are 'ill enough' to go to the doctor in the first place? **Zola** argues that friends and relatives are often important in interpreting something as a 'symptom' worthy of the doctor's attention. He also argues that patients' reasons for seeking medical help are affected by cultural background. His study in the USA found that Italians often sought help because symptoms interfered with personal relationships. Anglo-Saxons were more likely to seek help if symptoms affected their work, while the Irish were likely to present symptoms because of pressure from others to seek help.

Interactionists are interested in how doctors and patients **negotiate a diagnosis** (i.e. a sickness label). **Byrne and Long** found that there is a conflict between doctors' and patients' views of the ideal consultation (not surprisingly, doctors prefer short, doctor-centred consultations).

Doctors generally have more **power** in these interactions, but patients are not always passive and may try to create their own diagnosis and get the doctor to agree to it.

While the medical model equates **disability** with illness, sociologists generally see disability as socially constructed. We can distinguish between **impairment**, which involves loss of physical, sensory or intellectual functioning, for example, being partially sighted or lacking a limb, and **disability**, which refers to the restrictions society places on people who have impairments.

Using this distinction, **Shakespeare** argues that disability is a social and not a medical problem, stemming from society's failure to address the needs of people with impairments. In this view, disability is the result of discrimination. Social and environmental barriers exclude people with impairments from participation in mainstream society. **Society has disabling effects** when its buildings, education, employment and transport systems fail to meet the needs of people with impairments.

Impairment may have **social causes**. For example, accidents at work, poor quality housing, etc. can cause injury and disease. In general, manual workers and their families are at greater risk of impairment.

Mental illness

There are two main sociological approaches to the study of mental illness: the **positivist approach** and the **interactionist approach**.

- The **positivist** approach tends to accept medical definitions and assumes that mental illness is an objective 'thing' or disease. This approach examines the distribution of mental illness among different groups in society and seeks to discover its causes.

  For example, **Hollingshead and Redlich** show that members of class V were over six times more likely than members of class I to suffer from mental illness. **Faris and Dunham** found rates of mental illness were highest in areas of Chicago that had high levels of social disorganization. This approach traces mental illness to the way society is organized and the position of the individual in the social structure.

Feminists argue that the higher rates of mental illness among women are caused by their position in the social structure, for example, as a result of the stress factors associated with their domestic roles. Similarly, **racial discrimination** and disadvantage faced by **ethnic minorities** create stress and may result in higher rates of mental illness.

- The **interactionist** approach sees mental illness not as a disease or medical condition, but as a social construct: a label or social status conferred on some individuals by others (e.g. psychiatrists) who have the power to do so. Interactionists focus on the **labelling process** when someone is defined as mentally ill. For example, in **Rosenhan's** pseudo-patient experiment, the researchers gained admission to mental hospitals by claiming (falsely) to hear voices. Once admitted, they found that staff interpreted all their behaviour as symptoms of mental illness.

  Such labelling can create a **self-fulfilling prophecy**: once defined and treated as 'mentally ill', a person may begin to see themselves, and act, as mentally ill. **Goffman** describes how an individual's **identity** changes once admitted to a **total institution** such as a mental hospital. On admission, the individual's old identity is destroyed, and they are given the new identity of 'inmate'. Similarly, **Lemert** describes how labelling a person as **paranoid** creates a vicious circle where other people begin to avoid them; this isolates the person, increasing their paranoia.

  Szasz argues that mental illness is not really illness at all, but a label attached to individuals whose behaviour does not conform. In his view, psychiatry is a form of social control. **Scheff** sees differences in status and power as central to this labelling process: those who have least power are most likely to be labelled as mentally ill.

Women are more likely than men to be admitted to a mental hospital for almost all the major mental illnesses. This is partly because women are more likely to admit distress and define their problems in mental health terms. However, **feminists** argue that doctors tend to see female patients as hysterical and interpret women's physical symptoms as having psychological causes.

Pilgrim and Rogers describe how social judgements about deviance are influenced by gender stereotypes. Women are stereotyped as vulnerable and passive, so that when they are deviant (e.g. behaving aggressively), this is more likely to be seen as irrational and needing psychiatric treatment. Men's deviance is more likely to be seen as intentional and dangerous, and so they are more likely to be regarded as criminal than mentally ill.

Pilgrim and Rogers see stereotyping as the reason for the higher rate of mental illness among **Afro-Caribbeans**, especially young men. They are much more likely than their white counterparts to be labelled as dangerous by the police and courts and referred much more frequently for psychiatric assessments.

Check yourself

Health

Medicine and the medical profession

1 Define and give an example of 'iatrogenic illness'. (2)

2 What is meant by chronic illness? Give one example of a chronic illness. (2)

3 Which perspective or theory says that:

A 'Sickness is a form of deviance and so must be controlled'? (1)

B 'Doctors use their position to benefit themselves'? (1)

C 'Medicine plays an important part in maintaining patriarchal society'? (1)

4 Why does Parsons see doctors as able to control access to the sick role? (1)

5 According to Parsons, what rights and obligations does the sick role involve? (2)

6 Identify two of the functions that Marxists see medicine and the medical profession performing for capitalism. (2)

The social construction of health, illness and disability

1 Suggest two reasons why doctors have more power in consultations than patients. (2)

2 Explain the difference between impairment and disability. (2)

Mental illness

1 How might (**a**) a positivist and (**b**) an interactionist explain the differences in rates of mental illness between different ethnic groups? (2)

2 How might a feminist explain the higher rates of mental illness among women? (2)

The answers are on pages 110–11.

Perspectives on the mass media

Each perspective has a different explanation of the role of the media in society and about who controls the media and how it influences audiences.

- **Elite theory** is based on the view that a small organised minority – the elite – controls the media and uses it to **manipulate** the majority. This is also known as the theory of **mass society**, from which the term 'mass media' originates.
- **Pluralists** do not deny that elite groups exist, but argue that there are many different sources of information to choose from. In this view, it is the **consumers** (i.e. audiences) who hold the power.
- **Marxists** see the media as serving the interests of capitalism, as it is owned and controlled by the ruling class. The output of the media transmits a **dominant ideology** that disguises inequality and exploitation.
- **Interactionists** are interested in **labelling** processes and the effects of stereotypes. They have shown how negative labels created by the media can produce a spiral of deviance amplification.
- **Feminists** show how the media stereotypes women by casting them in traditional roles and by representing them as sex objects. The media serves the interests of **patriarchy**: men's power over women.
- **Postmodernists** believe we now live in a **media-saturated society**. We are surrounded by a vast range of images, styles and sources of information – a **media-scape** – from which we pick and mix elements to fashion our identities.

Some perspectives see control of the media as **concentrated** in a few hands and media output as having a direct influence on a **passive** audience. Others see control of the media as **diffused** and the audience as **active** and capable of choosing from the range of media sources available.

Ownership, control and output of the mass media

Sociologists are interested in the factors that shape the output of the mass media. For example, who is it that makes key decisions and how far can advertisers, consumers, big business or governments influence the output of the media?

Murdock shows that most of the media is now owned by large business corporations. Ownership has become more concentrated: mergers and take-overs have meant a trend towards **corporate control**. As a result, media companies have become part of large conglomerates owned by shareholders and controlled by managers and media professionals.

Pluralists argue that there has been a divorce between ownership and control. Companies used to be owned and controlled by an individual or family, but now shareholders are the legal owners of large companies, whilst day-to-day control rests with managers and professionals.

Pluralists believe in **consumer sovereignty**: the view that the consumer is king. Media corporations are geared to providing what the consumer wants, so it is ultimately the consumer who controls what media companies produce. This means that media professionals, such as editors and journalists, are aware of what their readers and viewers want and have to compete with each other for a share of the audience.

Marxists argue that the media serves the interests of the capitalist system. The media is no longer owned by individual capitalists, but power and control remain concentrated among top executives. Day-to-day control may be delegated to editors and journalists, but they operate within a capitalist environment and have to conform to the values of the companies they work for. Marxists therefore dismiss the idea of consumer sovereignty.

Murdock identifies two main types of Marxist explanation:

- **Instrumentalist** In this view the media justifies the position of the ruling class because it is owned by them. The ruling class uses the media as an instrument to maintain its power.
- **Structuralist** In this view the media is tied closely to the structure of capitalism. Media corporations are part of big business and run along capitalist lines. They have to make a profit and are controlled by the advertisers and the banks that finance them.

Curran's findings support the structuralist explanation. For example, the popular press avoids serious discussion of politics because a formula of sex, sport and scandal is more attractive to advertisers. Equally, editorial advice about investment planning in financial papers provides an attractive context for companies to advertise financial products.

The recent growth of **global and interactive media**, such as satellite, cable and the Internet, has greatly increased the number of media channels throughout the world. Pluralists see these developments as strengthening consumer sovereignty by extending choice. **Postmodernists** go further and argue that the difference between producers and consumers of the mass media is disappearing because new interactive media allow audiences to produce media messages themselves.

Murdock argues that these developments have not brought about fundamental changes in the relationship between ownership, control and what the media produce. The media is still owned mainly by western corporations and media output is aimed at western audiences. The demands of advertising and the need to appeal to large audiences restrict the range of programmes. Western audiences have more **access to the media** because they are better off.

Selection and presentation of news

Sociologists are interested in the causes of bias in the output of the media: how the mass media explains events, and the images of social groups it puts forward.

From a **Marxist** perspective, the **Glasgow University Media Group** identified the following sources of bias in television **news coverage of strikes** in the 1970s:

- **Biased vocabulary**: for example, union leaders are described as 'demanding' and 'making threats', but employers as 'pleading' and 'making offers'.
- **Selective reporting**: journalists are 'gate-keepers' who decide which stories to report and which to ignore or play down.
- **Emphasis on effects not causes**: reporting emphasizes the inconvenience caused by strikes while ignoring the underlying causes and the views of strikers.
- **Selective use of visuals**: for example, by interviewing employers in the calm surroundings of their offices, but union officials outside, in front of factory gates, where they have to shout to be heard.
- **Hierarchy of access**: reporters take employers and their views more seriously. Employers are presented as normal, sensible people acting in the public interest, but strikers and their leaders are described as unruly and easily led, and are portrayed as a disruptive minority.

From an **interactionist** perspective, **Cohen and Young** show that media coverage focuses on newsworthy **events and personalities**. They point to three types of study which help to explain the causes of bias in the news:

- **Studies comparing news coverage with official statistics** For example, **Roshier** shows that newspapers are selective and biased in the way they report crime news. Some types of crime are given more coverage then others, such as serious crimes, those which are humorous or have a human interest angle and crimes which involve famous people.

- **Studies linking stereotyping to the processes involved in newsgathering** **Galtung and Ruge** argue in relation to **foreign news** that the 24-hour news cycle and constant pressure for stories lead to an event and personality orientation which highlights dramatic incidents at the expense of background information.

- **Studies of deviance amplification** Cohen and Young show that the media create moral panics by focusing on newsworthy events. By focusing on deviant behaviour and **labelling** it, the media can provoke a negative reaction from the public, the police and other official agencies. This exaggerates the problem and sets a vicious circle in motion. **Cohen** shows this in his study of media coverage of the **mods and rockers**' disturbances of the 1960s.

Hall argues that the media plays an important but secondary role in this labelling process. There is a **hierarchy of credibility**, which means that journalists are more likely to believe information from official sources, such as the police or government, than information from other sources. Journalists are therefore **secondary definers** who rely on **primary definers** for their information. This means that the version of events presented by the media is likely to be the one provided by the police and other official agencies. Hall uses this framework to examine the moral panic about '**mugging**' in the 1970s.

Hall's view is challenged by recent studies. **McRobbie** notes that the media draws increasingly on a range of sources rather than relying on official sources alone. Minority groups often have experts and self-help groups to defend them. This adds a new dimension to moral panics, with claims and counter-claims and arguments that represent different points of view.

Postmodernists use the term **hyper-reality** to describe how images and reality merge. Images in the news vary widely in their relationship to what actually happened. This is apparent in news reports that present a **pastiche** of images to create a spectacle: the studio anchor, the reporter on the spot, documentary pictures, archive or amateur footage, expert opinion, artist's impressions and computer graphics.

Check yourself

Mass media

Perspectives on the mass media

1 Read statements **A–D** about the mass media and identify the perspective associated with each.

- **A** 'A small group of powerful individuals use the mass media to spread propaganda and brainwash the masses.' (1)
- **B** 'The output of the mass media reinforces traditional stereotypes of men and women.' (1)
- **C** 'Society is saturated with media images. People pick and mix from these images to create their own identities and styles.' (1)
- **D** 'The mass media serves the interests of the ruling class and capitalist system.' (1)

2 True or false? 'Pluralists believe that control of the mass media is concentrated in a few hands.' (1)

3 True or false? 'Interactionists are interested in the way the mass media labels deviance.' (1)

Ownership, control and output of the mass media

1 Explain what is meant by 'corporate control'. (1) Why is there a trend towards corporate control of the media? (1)

2 What do pluralists mean by 'consumer sovereignty'? (1)

3 Why do Marxists reject the idea of consumer sovereignty? (1)

4 Explain the difference between instrumentalist and structuralist explanations of the role of the media in capitalist society. (2)

5 Explain what is meant by 'global media' (1) and 'interactive media'. (1)

Check yourself

Selection and presentation of news

1. Write a paragraph about the findings of the Glasgow University Media Group using as many of the following terms as you can (in any order): biased vocabulary; selective use of visuals; hierarchy of access; Marxist perspective. (4)
2. What reason do Galtung and Ruge give for the emphasis on dramatic incidents in foreign news? (1)
3. Explain what sociologists mean by 'deviance amplification'. (1)
4. Why does Hall argue that the mass media play a secondary role in the labelling process? (1)
5. What, in McRobbie's view, has given moral panics a new dimension? (1)
6. Briefly define and illustrate what postmodernists mean by 'pastiche'. (2)

The answers are on pages 111–12.

Representations of social groups in the media

Studies of **representation** examine **images of social groups** in the media. News and documentaries provide some examples, but other areas are drama and sitcoms, music, magazines, cinema, etc.

In the 1980s, **Golding and Middleton** examined representations of **social class** in a study of the tabloid press. They found the press scapegoated benefit claimants, creating an atmosphere of 'scroungerphobia', which encouraged support for cutbacks in welfare spending. Another example is **Glennon and Butsch's** study of American sitcoms. Most families in sitcoms are shown as middle class or wealthy; when working class families are portrayed, they are portrayed either as upwardly mobile or as figures of fun.

Representations of ethnicity are explored in **Jhally and Lewis'** study of *The Cosby Show*. The show presents a comforting but unrepresentative image of a black American family – the Huxtables – who appear to be unaffected by problems of racism. The researchers argue that by representing black families in this way the programme, and others like it, mask the existence of racism. **Hartmann and Husband** adopt a different approach. Applying the deviance amplification model, they show how news and documentaries tend to focus on **ethnic minorities** mainly when they are in confrontation with authority. This results in stereotypes that perpetuate prejudice and discrimination.

Women's magazines have been a focal point for studies of **gender** in the media. **Ferguson** found that from 1949 to 1974 the magazines' main themes were love, marriage and self-improvement, reflecting a cult of **femininity**. By 1980, however, there was a new emphasis on self-esteem and mutual support, reflecting the struggle for women's independence. Women were not represented solely as housewives.

McRobbie observes a similar change of approach in magazines aimed at teenage girls. She sums this up in the contrast between *Jackie* in the 1970s and *Just Seventeen* in the 1990s. *Jackie* represented girls as passive and dependent, but in *Just Seventeen* they are represented as independent and self-confident.

Connell uses the term 'exemplary masculinity' to describe stereotyped images of the ideal man found in popular culture, such as sports programmes and Hollywood movies. These images are frequently linked to violence, for example, the Stallone or Schwarzenegger character, and their effect is to devalue other types of masculinity. Connell's analysis helps to explain why gay men and other **sexual minorities** are under-represented and stereotyped in the media. **Pearce** shows that the media almost always presents homosexuality as a problem or a threat. **Gross** argues that lesbians and gay men experience 'symbolic annihilation' by the media because it ignores their existence. Alternatively, the media portrays lesbians and gay men as ridiculous or pitiful.

Featherstone and Wernick examine **images of old age in the media**. They note that old age is represented as a period of dependency. Programmes like *Last of the Summer Wine* portray the elderly as going through a second childhood. Images of old age also reflect our culture's denial of illness and death. The subject of dying (as opposed to killing), is generally avoided in popular television. Magazines like *Retirement Choice* avoid the topics of illness and death by presenting an image of the 'young-old' enjoying their leisure time.

In relation to disability, **Cumberbatch and Negrine** showed that **people with disabilities** are under-represented on prime-time television programmes, news broadcasts and specialist programmes; none appeared in game shows or current affairs programmes and they were a tiny proportion of characters in dramas. **Darke** approaches the subject differently. Far from being invisible, he argues that disability is the main theme in films like *My Left Foot* and *Born on the First of July*, but that such films stereotype **disability** by presenting it as something mysterious involving tragedy and triumph.

The mass media and audience effects

Research on the effects of the media began in the 1940s against the background of fears about brainwashing and propaganda. In common with elite theory, the **hypodermic syringe model** suggests that audiences are passive and unable to resist media messages. This view is challenged by research evidence.

Lazersfeld's two-step flow model shows that people are not influenced directly by the media. He found in election campaigns that people interpret media messages through a framework of attitudes they acquire from primary groups and opinion leaders. **Katz** also rejects the idea that people are manipulated. His **uses and gratification model** suggests that individuals make selective use of the mass media to meet their needs for information and enjoyment.

From a review of research, **Klapper** concludes that the mass media is more likely to reinforce existing attitudes and behaviour than to change them. Our existing attitudes act as a **protective net** preventing any direct effect. It follows that the media has most influence when an audience lacks knowledge and clear opinions. **Halloran** believes that the media has most influence when individuals are socially isolated and when the audience lacks direct experience.

Deviance is an example of behaviour about which audiences often lack direct experience. This helps to explain why media coverage of deviance can create moral panics. The **effect of moral panics** is to reinforce the moral boundaries of society. From a functionalist point of view this creates social solidarity by reinforcing the shared values of the community, but Marxists argue that scapegoating of minority groups deflects attention from class inequality and protects the position of the powerful.

Hall's encoding/decoding model examines the relationship between media production and effects. Encoding describes the production of media messages. From a **Marxist perspective** media production serves the interests of the dominant class (see pages 30–1). The media transmits what **Althusser** calls the **dominant ideology**. Hall accepts this view of media output, but argues that audiences are not passive victims of the dominant ideology, but can decode media messages in different ways.

Hall's approach has been described as a hegemonic model because it is based on **Gramsci's** concepts of hegemony and counter-hegemony. Gramsci argues that the power of the dominant class is not absolute but provisional. The dominant class promotes its view of the world (i.e. its hegemony) through the media and in other ways, but comes up against varying degrees of opposition and resistance from below.

Morley tests the encoding-decoding model in his study of *Nationwide*, a television news programme. He showed recordings of the programme to audiences from different backgrounds and found differential de-codings, i.e. they de-coded the programmes in one of three different ways:

- **dominant de-codings** where audiences shared the world view of the programme-makers
- **negotiated de-codings** where audiences disagreed with some aspects of the programme
- **oppositional de-codings** where audiences rejected or ignored the programme altogether.

Oppositional de-codings are an example of what Gramsci described as **cultural resistance and counter-hegemony**. For example, a group of shop stewards in the study opposed the middle class bias of the programme and a group of black students rejected it as irrelevant.

Morley's follow-up study called 'Everyday Television' uncovers the 'politics of the living room' by studying television viewing in the context of people's homes. He found evidence of **gendered viewing**. For example, fathers appear to exert the most influence on the choice of family viewing.

Recent studies by the **Glasgow University Media Group** provide evidence of **alternative de-codings** which show that audiences are not passive recipients of media messages but that they interpret and construct them in a social context. Both **Kitzinger's study** of media portrayals or HIV/AIDS and **Philo's study** of audience responses to the 1984–5 miners' strike show that audiences do not receive media messages in a vacuum, but play an active part in constructing them.

However, the media has the power to structure people's thinking and set the agenda.

Feminist explanations of the effects of the media have changed. Early feminist approaches resembled the hypodermic syringe model in seeing women as victims of **patriarchal ideology**. However, as **Jones and Jones** observe, such explanations have given way to more complex ones that recognize that sections of the media, and women themselves, can play an active part in opposing patriarchy.

Abercrombie and Longhurst put forward a **postmodernist** explanation of the effects of the media. They argue that the nature of audiences has been transformed because we now live in a **media-saturated society**. Audiences have become fragmented. In postmodern society everyone is part of an audience almost all the time. Individuals and groups use the media as raw material to create their identities.

In postmodern society the difference between consumers (i.e. audiences) and producers is breaking down. Audiences now behave more like fans. Being part of an audience can mean adopting a certain attitude and personality. We can observe this in the fan following for fashion, musical styles and sci-fi programmes. However, it also applies to 'mainstream' areas such as sport, soap operas, DIY, gardening, etc.

Fiske recognizes the importance of the processes that postmodernists describe but argues that only the affluent few are in a position to afford a postmodern lifestyle. Similarly, Murdock stresses that we should not lose sight of economic constraints that restrict people's access to the media. Ownership of information and communication technology, including the Internet, varies greatly according to family income.

Check yourself

Mass media

Representations of social groups in the media

1 Name two studies of representations of social class in the media. (2)

2 Explain the difference between Jhally and Lewis' findings and Hartmann and Husband's findings about representations of ethnicity in the media. (2)

3 According to Ferguson, how have representations of women changed? (1)

4 Explain what is meant by 'exemplary masculinity' and 'symbolic annihilation'. (2)

5 Featherstone and Wernick identify two main images of old age in the media. What are they? (2)

6 Explain the difference between Cumberbatch and Negrine's analysis and Darke's analysis of images of disability. (2)

The mass media and audience effects

1 True or false? 'The hypodermic model suggests that the mass media has a direct effect on audiences.' (1)

2 Suggest two reasons why people are not influenced directly by the media. (2)

3 Explain what Marxists see as the main effect of moral panics. (1)

4 Write a paragraph about the encoding/decoding model using as many of the following terms as you can (in any order): encoding; decoding; dominant ideology; differential de-codings. (4)

5 Identify one way in which feminist explanations of the effects of the media have changed. (1)

The answers are on pages 112–13.

Class differences in educational achievement

On average, pupils from middle class backgrounds stay longer in full-time education and achieve better qualifications at all levels than pupils from working class backgrounds. Despite the expansion of state education and continuing improvements in the overall level of educational achievement, class differences in achievement persist.

Great Britain	Percentages	
	1991–92	1998–99
Professional	55	72
Intermediate	36	45
Skilled non-manual	22	29
Skilled manual	11	18
Partly skilled	12	17
Unskilled	6	13
All social classes	23	31

Participation rates in higher education by social class

Some explanations focus on external causes, i.e. factors outside the education system. Others focus on internal causes, i.e. processes within the education system itself.

Douglas identifies the major external causes of working class under-achievement as **cultural and material deprivation**. His study traces working class failure to factors in a child's home background such as lack of achievement motivation (i.e. lack of encouragement from parents), and poor housing conditions. **Linguistic deprivation** has also been identified as a cause. **Bernstein** distinguishes between restricted and elaborated codes of speech, suggesting that children from working class backgrounds are less successful in education because they lack the ability to understand and express abstract ideas.

The above explanations reflect a **functionalist** point of view. Inadequate socialization by the family is seen as the main cause of failure. Those who fail do so because they are deprived of the pre-school experiences and motivation which success requires.

Compensatory education is seen as a way to reduce inequalities in education. Government policies have aimed to compensate children for the inadequacies of their home backgrounds by providing extra funds for deprived areas. Education Action Zones are an example.

Keddie argues that the **myth of cultural deprivation** blames working class families for educational failure, but the real reason is that the education system fails to meet their needs. Schools are middle class institutions that fail to recognize and respond to any culture other than their own.

Becker's research shows that teachers have an image of **the ideal pupil** that equates to being middle class. He found teachers perceived working class pupils as lacking motivation and difficult to control.

Positive and negative labels can act as a **self-fulfilling prophecy** that affects children's self-image and academic performance. Those labelled negatively tend to deteriorate while those labelled positively improve.

Keddie develops these themes in her study of 'classroom knowledge'. Alongside the formal curriculum (i.e. the subjects that are officially taught) is a **hidden curriculum** that operates at an informal level. This consists of the hidden ways in which pupils are expected to conform to middle class standards, such as being interested in knowledge for its own sake.

Pupil sub-cultures are another source of class inequality. **Lacey's study** of Hightown Grammar shows how streaming can lead to the formation of an anti-school culture, with negative effects on the achievements of pupils in low streams. **Ball's study** of Beachside Comprehensive found that even when streaming was replaced by mixed ability grouping, teachers continued to have low expectations of working class pupils.

The above explanations, which focus on processes within schools, reflect an **interactionist** perspective that rejects the idea of cultural deprivation. In this view, working class children are put at a disadvantage by a system that judges them according to middle class standards.

Marxists criticize interactionists for producing small-scale studies without linking them to a broader explanation of the nature of inequality in capitalist society. Marxists focus on how the education system reproduces class inequalities. They argue that processes within schools are closely linked to the workings of the capitalist economy.

A key question for recent research is whether the **1988 Education Reform Act (ERA)** has brought about an increase in choice and, if so, which social groups have benefited. Key features of the 1988 Education Reform Act include:

- A **National Curriculum** for children of compulsory school age in the maintained sector, accompanied by **standardized tests** (SATs)
- **Local Management of Schools** (LMS), under which headteachers and governors of schools have greater control over their school's budget
- Permission for schools to have **open enrolment**
- A scheme under which schools are allowed to **opt out** of local authority control and become grant-maintained
- **League tables** of schools' exam performance.

A major study by **Gewirtz et al** found that middle-class parents – being better off and better educated themselves – can exercise more choice about which schools their children attend. Middle class parents have cultural and economic capital; they are therefore skilled at seeking out successful schools and can afford the cost of travelling to selective schools. Working class parents, being restricted financially and less skilled at exploiting the available choices, are likely to opt for local schools. Pressures on schools to improve league table scores reinforce these inequalities. Thus education since ERA continues to reproduce the relative advantages of the middle class.

Walford et al's study of City Technology Colleges and **Fitz et al's study** of Grant Maintained schools show that ERA reinforced traditional and selective forms of education rather than extending diversity and choice. Ball concludes that the National Curriculum reinforces traditional forms of education.

Bartlett and LeGrand observe that market forces have led to **cream-skimming** and **silt-shifting**. Schools are under pressure to attract academically able pupils and to shift responsibility for less able pupils elsewhere. **Whitty** observes that the pressure to improve league table scores and maximize government funding has reinforced inequality. Popular schools can afford to screen out pupils from disadvantaged backgrounds, whereas under-subscribed schools are obliged to take them. Such pressures have led to the **re-introduction of selection**, which puts working class pupils at a disadvantage.

Since ERA, government concern has focused on the need to improve 'failing schools'. However, **Mortimore and Whitty's** findings suggest that while 'schools can make some difference' to levels of educational achievement, the major cause of under-achievement is poverty.

Ethnic differences in educational achievement

Sociological research has challenged the view that ethnic differences in achievement reflect innate differences of intelligence and ability. Very few social scientists now put forward such explanations. Explanations emphasize environmental factors either in a child's home and cultural background, or within the education system itself. Recent studies highlight the effects of racism.

Bereiter et al put forward **cultural and linguistic deprivation** as an explanation of the below average achievement of ethnic minority pupils. They see the culture and language of ethnic minority groups as deficient and children from such backgrounds as lacking the background knowledge and experience required for success at school.

Against this view, **Baratz and Baratz** argue that ethnic minority children are not culturally deprived, but culturally different. They are put at a disadvantage by an education system that fails to recognize their culture. This view is supported by **Labov's study**, which shows that the language spoken by black children in New York is different to Standard English but not inferior.

Another major problem with explanations based on cultural deprivation is that they do not distinguish between different ethnic minority groups. However, as **Gillborn** has found, there are considerable differences in levels of achievement between ethnic groups (see below).

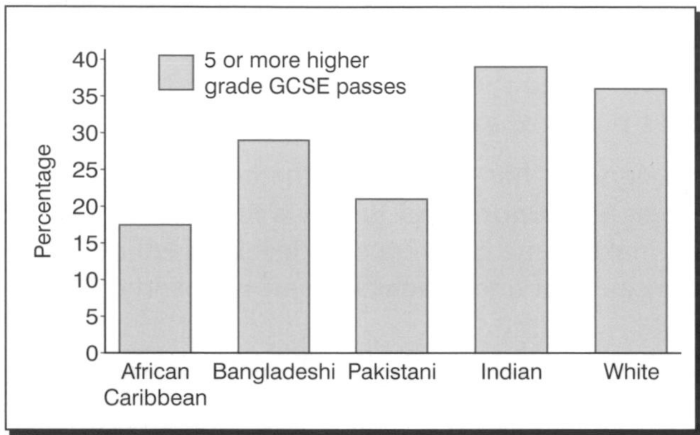

Ethnic origin and GCSE attainment for both sexes, Birmingham (1995)

Pryce suggests that the different levels of achievement of Asian compared with African Caribbean pupils are due to cultural differences and not cultural deprivation. He believes that African Caribbean culture, language and family life were damaged by slavery. By contrast, Asian culture and family structure remained stronger despite the effects of British colonial rule. **Driver** also emphasizes cultural differences. Comparing the educational achievements of West Indian girls and boys, he found that the girls were more successful and attributed this to the matrifocal family structure of West Indian communities.

The above explanations have attracted criticism. **Lawrence** argues that Pryce merely puts forward a version of cultural deprivation that ignores the strengths of African Caribbean culture. **Mirza** argues that the real explanation for low achievement is **racism** and not cultural differences or family structure.

Studies that focus on the internal workings of schools point to the effects of labelling, the hidden curriculum and pupil sub-cultures.

Wright found that primary teachers were **ethnocentric**: they disregarded Asian customs and assumed Asian children had language problems. Meanwhile, they perceived African Caribbean children as disruptive and a potential threat.

Evidence of discrimination is given in the **Commission for Racial Equality's** study of Jayleigh Comprehensive. This research found that Asian pupils were put in lower sets because of assumptions that teachers made about their abilities.

Studies of **pupil sub-cultures** have helped to challenge stereotypes of African Caribbean pupils. For example, **Fuller's study** of black girls in a London comprehensive shows that pupils can keep a positive self-image and achieve educational success despite the negative way they are sometimes labelled by teachers.

Sewell's research shows that the stereotype of the black macho lad applies only to a minority of pupils. Most African Caribbean boys in the school he studied were not rebels but conformists. Sewell concludes that racism is a more significant cause of under-achievement than membership of pupil sub-cultures.

Mirza has examined the **effects of racism** in education. She found evidence of widespread negative attitudes towards black pupils. She found that teachers' negative stereotypes of black pupils did not undermine their ambitions or self-esteem. However, racism limited their opportunities by restricting their access to teachers' time, unbiased careers advice and learning materials. The girls used strategies to avoid racism, such as being selective about which members of staff to ask for help and avoiding certain option choices, but this was at a cost to their progress.

Mirza identifies teachers as a vital link in the transmission of social and racial inequality. For example, although many black pupils had high aspirations, they were given careers advice which reflected teachers' low expectations of them.

Advocates of ERA (see page 44) believed that local management of schools would give more control to parents and local communities, including ethnic minority communities. However, **Deem** shows that decision-making on **school governing bodies** has stayed in the hands of headteachers and financial experts. **Hatcher et al** found that school governing bodies were dominated by white social networks; governors were unaware of race issues and few channels existed through which ethnic minority parents could express their concerns.

Ball describes how the introduction of the National Curriculum involved a process of **cultural restorationism** which underlined the value of English culture, history and language while marginalizing the cultures of ethnic minorities.

The National Curriculum demands that all pupils – whatever their cultural backgrounds – should be educated into the culture of the host community. For example, there is a lack of provision for minority languages and a strong emphasis on Christianity in the National Curriculum, with minimal recognition of other cultures. **Gillborn** describes this as **depluralization**: a process that restricts the scope for multi-cultural education and reinforces existing inequalities.

Gender differences in educational achievement

Since the mid-1980s, girls have caught up and overtaken boys, first at GCSE and now also at AS and A level. GCSE results from 1992 show that 46 per cent of girls but only 37 per cent of boys achieved five or more A–C grades. A study by **Arnot et al** shows that between 1984 and 1994, girls improved their performance relative to boys in GCSE exams, but boys continued to perform better at A level. In 2001, however, girls achieved better AS and A level results than boys.

This closing of the gender gap took place during a period when GCSE and A level results improved considerably for both sexes. It is important to recognize that boys' achievements also improved over this period. Media coverage has often confused the issue by presenting it as a problem of 'failing boys'.

Apart from exam results, other gender differences remain. **Coffey** argues that we should also look at gender in education in relation to the following:

- **Gender routes**: differences in the subjects that boys and girls study in schools
- **Gender relationships**: the role models available to boys and girls in schools
- **Gender regimes**: the way social control operates along gender lines in schools.

There continues to be an **arts-science divide** in the subjects that boys and girls study. There is also, however, considerable overlap.

Early studies, conducted at a time when girls were doing less well than boys, examined reasons for differences in subject choice and the apparent under-achievement of girls. Such studies are useful when seen in relation to changes that have taken place since.

Lobban's analysis of school **reading schemes** showed that they contained hidden messages about gender-appropriate behaviour. They depicted a female world of housework and childcare and a male world of work and activities outside the home.

Another theme is the hidden curriculum. The girls **Spender** interviewed believed it was natural for boys to ask questions and demand explanations and for girls to get on with their work. Teachers gave priority to boys and gave the impression that what girls said was less interesting and less important.

Stanworth found that boys dominated classroom interaction. Girls were on the margins. Teachers perceived girls as lower in a **sexual hierarchy of worth** and gave them less attention, discriminating against them unconsciously. This undermined the girls' self-confidence. This explains why the girls in Stanworth's study tended to under-estimate their abilities compared with the boys, who frequently over-estimated theirs.

Psycho-social explanations of gender differences focus on the process of **gender socialization**. An early example is **Maccoby and Jacklin's explanation** of differences in mathematical ability. In this view, boys and girls acquire different abilities through socialization within the home. Boys are taught to be active and expect change, where girls are rewarded for conformity. Maccoby and Jacklin suggest this is why boys develop an aptitude for maths and problem-solving and why girls get better results in tests of verbal ability.

Arnot et al describe the improvement in girls' achievement as 'progress against the odds'. It took place against the background of a backlash against feminism and right-wing government policies.

Weiner notes that despite opposition, feminists have played an active part in changing attitudes in education and society. Their efforts were supported during the 1980s by equal **opportunity initiatives** funded by Local Education Authorities (LEAs). Teachers challenged gender stereotypes, for example, by removing sexist images from teaching materials and by encouraging girls to want careers. Meanwhile, the appointment of more women to senior positions in schools has offered girls positive role models.

Other policies introduced in the 1980s helped to close the gender gap, although this was not their main aim. Girls benefited from the **introduction of GCSE**, which brought in new kinds of assessment, such as coursework. Despite less government support for equal opportunities after ERA, the **National Curriculum** reduced the influence of gender by making more subjects compulsory. The pressure to improve league table scores has also made schools keen to recruit girls who they perceive as high achievers and more amenable than boys.

Broader social and economic changes have also had an influence. Jobs in manufacturing industries have declined, bringing male unemployment; however, women's employment has increased. Some suggest this has undermined the traditional role of male breadwinner and head of household. More significantly, girls are now much less likely to see their future roles as housewives.

Interviews conducted by **Sharpe** show how girls' priorities have changed. In 1974, they were 'love, marriage, husbands and careers, more or less in that order', but by 1996, they were 'job, career and being able to support themselves'.

Many recent studies of gender differences in educational achievement have examined gender routes: the reasons why, on average, boys perform better at mathematical subjects while girls do better at arts subjects. Research suggests that gender preferences are not the result of different abilities, but stem from learned differences in motivation. **Browne and Ross** suggest that boys and girls tend to choose different subjects at school because early childhood experiences make them more confident about activities that fall within their own gender domains. These differences are reinforced by the way teachers respond to them.

Epstein explains that girls, on average, achieve better results in English because they are more familiar with the kind of imaginative and story-based material in reading schemes. They are more successful with GCSE English coursework because it demands descriptive writing and not information. Boys are more used to information texts. **Murphy and Elwood** found that boys are more confident with **scientific equipment** in school because they are more likely to play with electrical equipment and gadgets at home.

Other studies have explored gender relationships and gender regimes. Gender relationships include the different role models available to boys and girls. More women are now recruited into senior positions in schools than previously, but men still occupy most of these posts. School governors are mostly men, but 'dinner ladies' and most cleaners are women.

Mac an Ghaill describes how **gender regimes** in schools operate through an informal hierarchy which gives high status to heterosexual masculinity, but devalues femininity and subordinate forms of masculinity. It is evident in the way teachers control male pupils; for example, accusing boys in low streams of acting like girls, or teasing boys in high streams when girls do better. These observations show that gender inequalities in education remain significant.

Check yourself

Education

Class differences in educational achievement

1 True or false? 'The gap in the proportion of students from different class backgrounds in higher education has closed despite an overall reduction in the number of students in higher education.' (1)

2 Write a paragraph about the external causes of working class under-achievement using as many of the following terms as you can (in any order): external factors; cultural deprivation; functionalist perspective; cultural deprivation is a myth. (4)

3 Explain what sociologists mean by 'self-fulfilling prophecy'. (1)

4 Suggest two ways in which schools put working class pupils at a disadvantage. (2)

5 Briefly identify three key features of the 1988 Education Reform Act. (3)

6 Suggest two reasons why parents who are better off and better educated themselves have more choice within the state education system. (2)

7 What do Bartlett and LeGrand mean by 'cream-skimming' and 'silt-shifting'? (2)

Ethnic differences in educational achievement

1 Summarize what the chart on page 53 tells us about the percentage of pupils from each ethnic background that gained five or more higher grade passes at GCSE. (5)

2 Explain why it is important to distinguish between ethnic minority groups when examining differences in educational achievement. (1)

3 How does Pryce explain the different achievement levels of African Caribbean and Asian pupils? (1)

Check yourself

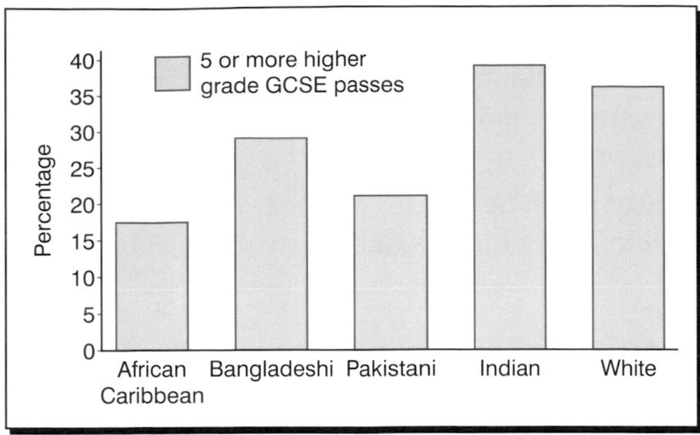

Ethnic origin and GCSE attainment for both sexes, Birmingham (1995)

4 How does Driver explain the higher achievements of West Indian girls compared to West Indian boys? (1)

5 Give one reason why Wright describes the teachers in her study as ethnocentric. (1)

6 Explain how racism limited black pupils' opportunities in the schools Mirza studied. (1)

7 Write a paragraph about ERA and ethnic differences in education using as many of the following terms as you can (in any order): local management of schools; school governing bodies; decision-making; white social networks; National Curriculum; depluralization. (6)

Gender differences in educational achievement

1 True or false? 'The gender gap in achievement closed because boys' achievements deteriorated.' (1)

2 Suggest two reasons why boys tend to dominate in classroom discussion. (2)

3 Explain why Arnot sees the improvement in girls' achievements as 'progress against the odds'. (1)

Check yourself

4 Suggest four changes within education that have helped to improve girl's achievements. (4)

5 Give two reasons why girls are now less likely to see their future roles as housewives. (2)

6 What do sociologists mean by gender routes? (1) How do they explain gender preferences for arts and science subjects? (1)

The answers are on pages 113–15.

Perspectives on the role of education in society

- The **functionalist perspective** is based on the view that each part of society, such as the family, education system and economy, performs functions that maintain society as a whole.

  Durkheim argues that education creates **social solidarity** by integrating individuals into a shared culture. Education also prepares individuals for their positions in the division of labour by teaching the skills required in work and industry.

  Like Durkheim, Parsons identifies **socialization** and **social integration** as key functions, but puts more emphasis on the need for social selection and role allocation. Schools are agencies of secondary socialization that transmit skills and values. Like **Davis and Moore**, he argues that the American education system is a **meritocracy**, i.e. selection and rewards are based on ability and effort.

- From a **Marxist perspective**, education must be understood in relation to the workings of the capitalist economy.

  Marxists **Bowles and Gintis** argue that education in a capitalist society reproduces and legitimizes social inequality. Firstly, schools **reproduce** a workforce with the skills that are needed at different levels of the capitalist economy. Secondly, they legitimize the inequalities they produce by making them seem fair and natural.

  Bowles and Gintis put forward these key concepts:
  - **The correspondence principle** Education exists in 'the long shadow of work'. Schools resemble offices and factories. Schools, like factories, are based on a system of top-down control and the hidden curriculum rewards conformity.
  - **The hierarchical division of labour** Selection and streaming in schools reproduces workers for different levels of the production process.
  - **The myth of meritocracy** The education system is a giant myth-making machine, which convinces people that social positions are based on merit, when in fact they are pre-determined by class background.

MacDonald criticizes Bowles and Gintis for ignoring gender inequality. From a **feminist perspective** she argues that schools reproduce both capitalism and **patriarchy**. Gender divisions in schools correspond to gender divisions in employment. The school hierarchy mirrors the control of women by male managers in the workplace.

Willis' study of 'the lads' – a group of working class rebels in a comprehensive school – is similar to Bowles and Gintis' approach in emphasizing the close relationship between education and work. Both adopt a Marxist approach. However, Willis stresses the importance of 'the lads' **counter culture** and the shop-floor culture it reflects. Willis sees the working class as capable of resisting the dominant ideology, including the education system. Unlike Bowles and Gintis, who see the education system as all-powerful, Willis sees 'the lads'' counter culture as evidence of a class struggle and of working class resistance.

Bourdieu also sees the education system as reproducing and legitimizing social inequality. However, he attaches central importance to **cultural capital**. He argues that the education system reproduces inequality by taking for granted that all children have cultural capital that in reality only middle class families possess. The result is that working class pupils are eliminated from the system. Education also legitimizes social inequality by making its origins appear to be based on individual ability.

- **New Right perspectives** are completely different to the perspectives outlined above. They gained popularity from the 1980s, among politicians rather than sociologists, and helped to shape the 1988 Education Reform Act. New Right beliefs about education can be summarized as follows:
  - Greater diversity of types of schools
  - Freedom of choice based on the rights of parents as consumers
  - Local control of schools without interference from the state
  - Excellence achieved through competition.

These opinions are echoed in the views of American political scientists **Chubb and Moe**, who argue that **parent power** and **community control** will make schools more efficient.

- **Postmodernists** offer another view of the role of education. They argue that society has become fragmented and that old divisions and hierarchies have broken down. There are many different and overlapping sources of identity, none of which are more significant than others.

  Usher and Edwards argue that education is becoming more diverse and tailored to the needs of particular communities and groups. It no longer performs functions for society as a whole.

  In an assessment of New Right and postmodernist views, Whitty argues that we need to recognize both continuity and change in education. In common with Giddens, he uses the term **late modern** rather than **postmodern** to describe our society. Rejecting New Right and postmodernist views of education he argues that education continues to reproduce and legitimize social inequality, but in less obvious ways.

  Ball develops similar themes, arguing that although ERA appeared to give power to schools and local communities, in practice it introduced **new and subtler forms of control**, including the National Curriculum, formula funding and league tables. These controls encourage schools to be selective and concentrate on high ability pupils. As a result, schools tend to reproduce the relative advantages of the middle class.

  Walford suggests that the ideology of consumer choice acts as **a new form of legitimation**. The idea of choice disguises the re-introduction of eductional selection. Choice is a practical option for only a privileged minority of parents and children, and serves to obscure the real reasons for failure in education. Failure is blamed on 'bad parenting' or 'failing schools', when the real reasons are social deprivation and poverty.

Education

Perspectives on the role of education in society

1 Read the following statements (**A–D**) and identify the perspective associated with them.

A 'The main function of education is to promote social solidarity.' (1)

B 'Selection in education is based on merit; in other words effort plus ability.' (1)

C 'Society is now much more diverse and fragmented. Education means different things to different individuals and communities.' (1)

D 'Parent power and community control make schools more efficient and responsive to local needs.' (1)

2 According to Bowles and Gintis, how do schools reproduce and legitimize social inequality? (2)

3 Why do Bowles and Gintis describe education as being 'in the long shadow of work'? (1)

4 What is MacDonald's main criticism of Bowles and Gintis? (1)

5 Explain why Ball rejects the suggestion that ERA gave local communities more control of schools. (1)

6 Explain Walford's argument that consumer choice in education is a new form of legitimation. (1)

The answers are on pages 115–16.

Wealth and income

Wealth refers to the value of the possessions held by an individual or group. **Income** is a flow of resources. It can be earned or unearned, either in the form of salaries, wages, pensions, benefits or interest from savings.

There are two main ways of **measuring the distribution of wealth**: the survey method and the estates method. The survey method involves asking people how much they own, while the estates method looks at how much the dead have left in their estate. Both methods tend to underestimate the extent of wealth. Respondents to surveys may play down the true extent of their wealth and statistics about inheritance tax tell us little about the extent of wealth owned by people who are alive or the extent of tax evasion. Ownership of **wealth** is concentrated among a small number of individuals and families. Home ownership has increased, but relatively few people possess large amounts of capital in the form of shares or other investments.

United Kingdom	**Percentages**			
Marketable wealth	1976	1986	1996	1998
Percentage of wealth owned by adults aged 18 and over				
Most wealthy 1%	21	18	20	23
Most wealthy 5%	38	36	40	44
Most wealthy 10%	50	50	52	56
Most wealthy 25%	71	73	74	75
Most wealthy 50%	92	90	93	94
Total marketable wealth (£ billion)	280	955	2,092	2,543

Ownership of wealth in the UK between 1976 and 1998

The table shows that in 1998 the most wealthy 1 per cent of individuals owned between a fifth and a quarter of total wealth. By contrast, half the population shared between them only 6 per cent of total wealth.

Drawing on evidence from the Family Expenditure Survey, **Devine** shows that since 1979 the share of **income** taken by the top 20 per cent of earners has risen, while the share taken by the bottom 20 per cent of earners has fallen.

The overall **effect of income tax** is progressive, that is, it takes a bigger proportion of the income of the rich than of the poor. However, since the 1980s, higher earners have benefited from much bigger tax cuts than average and low earners.

Poorer groups receive more in benefits, but it is also true that benefits to high-income groups are less visible than those to the poor. Dean and Taylor-Gooby note that by the late 1980s, private pensions, medical insurance, education and mortgages were subsidized to the tune of £24 billion annually. Higher income groups also gain most from the NHS and state education, for example, their children stay in education longer and gain higher qualifications.

The gender gap in income has remained fairly constant since the early 1970s, with women on average earning from 70 to 80 per cent of what men earn. Measures based on household income often conceal further inequalities between individuals in the same household, i.e. women often receive a smaller share of household income than men.

Adonis and Pollard describe Britain as an increasingly polarized society, firstly because **a new elite** has emerged since the 1960s based on the growth of legal, corporate and financial services, and secondly, because of taxation policy and privatization during and since the 1980s.

Functionalists believe that the importance of inherited *wealth* as a source of status declines when societies industrialize. Modern societies are meritocratic (i.e. social positions are determined by ability and effort). However, Davis and Moore argue that differences of *income* are necessary to ensure that the most talented people are attracted to the most functionally important occupations. Unequal incomes act as an incentive and ensure efficient role allocation, both of which are necessary in an industrial society with a complex division of labour.

Marxists argue that wealth and poverty are closely linked. **Marx** observed that capitalism creates, on the one hand, a world of wealth, and on the other, a world of poverty. Through their **ownership of capital**, the capitalist class exploit the labour of the majority, who face the threat of poverty as a result. In this view, capitalism is a machine for the systematic production of both wealth and poverty.

Poverty: definitions and measurement

There are two main ways to define and measure poverty:

- **Absolute poverty** is defined as a lack of the minimum required for human survival and is based on a measure of subsistence.
- **Relative poverty** is defined in relation to inequality and measured in relation to the standard of living in a particular society.

Using an absolute definition, **Rowntree** found that absolute poverty declined from 33 per cent in 1899 to 1.5 per cent in 1950 because of an improvement in the standard of living.

The absolute definition is criticized for being unrealistic. It assumes that the poverty line is universal, i.e. the same in all societies. In practice, however, standards differ culturally and historically. It also assumes that the poor have knowledge about diet and nutrition that only experts possess.

A relative definition sees poverty in relation to **social inequality**. What counts as poverty is relative to the standard of living and depends on social expectations. This view sees human needs as socially constructed, therefore new needs and expectations are created as the standard of living rises. To be in relative poverty means to lack the resources most people consider normal. The poor experience **social exclusion**: they are denied the right to participate in the life of the community.

Based on a relative definition, **Townsend's 1968 study** defines households with 50 per cent or less of average earnings as poor. Those on 50–80 per cent of average earnings are on the margins of poverty. He also uses a **deprivation index** to measure relative deprivation in education, health and diet, housing and working conditions, leisure and family life. He found a close link between relative deprivation and low income. Twenty-three per cent of the population were found to be in relative poverty.

Mack and Lansley put forward a **consensual definition** of poverty based on public perceptions. They found that people agreed about which items were essential and devised an index based on these. Direct comparisons with Townsend's findings are not possible – they use different measurements – but Mack and Lansley report an increase in numbers in poverty from 7.5 million in 1983 to 11 million in 1990.

The **composition of the poor** has changed. Sociologists distinguish between new poverty and old poverty. **Room** identifies the following changes:

- The **elderly** are now a smaller proportion of the poor.
- The unemployed have become a larger proportion of the poor. **Unemployment** and insecure employment have become the main cause of poverty.
- **Lone-parent families** have increased and become a larger proportion of the poor.
- From the 1970s, **homelessness**, **debt** and the proportion of families on **low incomes** also increased.

Poverty is more likely to afflict women, working class people and members of ethnic minorities throughout their lives and especially in childhood and old age. Vulnerability to poverty depends on an individual's position in the social structure, and especially on their position in the labour market.

Government statistics show similar trends. **LIF statistics** (Low Income Families) show a rise in the numbers living on or below the Income Support level, from 14% of the population in 1979 to 24% in 1992. When we add people just above Income Support level, we find that those living in poverty or on the margins of poverty increased from 24% to 33% of the population between 1979 and 1992. **HBAI statistics** (Households Below Average Incomes) show a similar increase in relative poverty and a widening gap between average incomes and the incomes of the poor.

Explanations of poverty

Graham divides explanations of poverty into two broad types: victim-blaming and system-blaming explanations:

- **Victim-blaming explanations** suggest that the poor themselves are to blame for their poverty. They see the cause of poverty as lying in the moral character of individuals or the culture of the poor as a group. The explanations include the culture of poverty thesis, individual explanations and New Right versions of underclass theory.
- **System-blaming explanations** suggest that poverty is not the fault of the poor, but of the social system in which they live. The wider structure of social inequality is seen as the cause of poverty.

Lewis' culture of poverty thesis suggests the poor have a distinctive sub-culture, with different values from mainstream society. They lack ambition and have short-term goals, living for today and not planning for the future. This culture is transmitted to the young through socialization, keeping them in poverty.

Coates and Silburn reject this view. They found that poor people in Nottingham had the same culture and ambitions as everyone else, but were denied opportunities because of their class position. In this view, the hopelessness and despair felt by the poor is a *result* of poverty and not its cause.

Individual explanations attribute poverty to irresponsibility and laziness. This view draws on Victorian ideas about self-reliance and self-help which Mrs Thatcher's Conservative governments in the 1980s revived. **Marsland** believes that welfare benefits have undermined the will to work and created a **culture of dependency**. In this view, the poor are individuals who lack the ability to be self-reliant. Individual explanations have been described as unsociological. They blame the poor themselves and fail to recognize the impact of wider social forces, including discrimination, economic re-structuring and government policy.

Saunders describes **the underclass** as a stratum of people who are generally poor, unqualified and irregularly or never employed. New Right thinkers such as Murray believe that members of the underclass 'live in a different world' with distinctive behaviour patterns and attitudes reflected in a high rate of juvenile delinquency, single-parent families and preference for benefits rather than work. These problems, he believes, are caused by **over-generous welfare benefits** and the reduced stigma attached to divorce and births outside marriage.

Murray's views have attracted criticism for their vagueness, bias and lack of research evidence supporting them.

Dean and Taylor-Gooby found little evidence to support the idea of an underclass amongst the benefit claimants they studied. Most of the claimants they interviewed were **reluctant dependents**: they wanted to work and had similar attitudes to people in employment.

Likewise in a large-scale survey, **Marshall et al** found little difference of attitude between the poor and non-poor or the employed and unemployed. Furthermore, they did not find evidence of an underclass with the kind of attitudes that Murray describes.

Devine concludes that 'the poor are not the perpetrators of their own predicament. On the contrary, **the rise in poverty needs to be located in a structural context**, namely the manufacturing decline and substantial job loss in both the USA and Britain.'

System-blaming explanations link poverty to social structure and inequality. Coates and Silburn argue that the poor are kept poor by **situational constraints**, i.e. the limits imposed by their economic circumstances. In this view, the solution to poverty is a fundamental re-distribution of wealth and not a reduction in welfare benefits as advocated by the New Right.

Weber's theory of class, status and power has been used as a framework for explaining poverty, for example, by Townsend. For Weber, an individual's **class position** is greatly influenced by whether they have **marketable skills**. This explains why unskilled manual workers and their families are at greatest risk of poverty caused by low pay and unemployment. It also explains why women and ethnic minorities, who are more likely to be unskilled, are over-represented among the poor.

Status position results from the way a group or individual is perceived by others. Such perceptions can be positive or negative. Groups that are perceived negatively are likely to experience **discrimination** that limits their opportunities, for example, in employment. Such groups include ethnic minorities, women, lone parents, the elderly, disabled and unemployed. They are more vulnerable to poverty because of the discrimination they face. **Rex and Tomlinson** explain the status position of **ethnic minorities** in these terms.

The poor also lack power because they lack bargaining power and are not politically organized. For example, they are not represented by trade unions or professional associations and the policies of major political parties tend to be aimed at middle income groups. Thus the poor are a group over whom others – such as employers and landlords – exercise power, rather than a group that exercises power over others.

Oppenheim notes that **women** are over-represented among the poor. Women are more likely than men to be low-paid and part-time workers, and a large proportion of lone parents and the elderly are women. Measures of poverty based on household income disguise the true extent of poverty amongst women. Women often sacrifice their own needs to ensure their families' needs are met.

For **Marxists**, poverty is a product of capitalism and the poor are part of the working class, not a separate group or underclass below it. Capitalist profits depend on keeping wages low, and this causes poverty. All workers face the risk of poverty. People don't become poor simply because they are old or sick or lone parents, but because of their **class position**. Working class people are vulnerable to poverty because they have no other source of income than their own labour, which they must sell to the capitalist class to survive.

Marxists argue that **poverty performs several functions for the capitalist system**:

- Poverty and **low wages** help to keep the general level of wages down.
- Fear of poverty is a form of **social control**. It makes the workforce willing to accept badly paid and unfulfilling jobs.
- By **dividing the working class** into employed and unemployed, well and badly paid, poverty prevents the working class from uniting to overthrow capitalism.

Check yourself

Wealth, poverty and welfare

Wealth and income

1. Identify the two main methods used to measure the distribution of wealth. (2)
2. True or false? 'Regressive taxation redistributes income and wealth from the rich to the poor.' (1)
3. Give two examples of how state welfare provision has benefited the rich. (2)
4. Explain why measurements of poverty based on household income tend to underestimate the extent of poverty amongst women. (1)
5. Suggest two reasons why, according to Adonis and Pollard, Britain has become a more polarized society. (2)
6. What reason do Davis and Moore give to support their view that income differences are necessary? (1)

Poverty: definitions and measurement

1. Briefly explain the difference between absolute and relative poverty. (2)
2. Explain what is meant by the statement 'human needs are socially constructed'. (1)
3. Explain how Mack and Lansley define and measure poverty. (2)
4. Name three categories of people who are likely to be poor. (3)
5. True or false? 'Poverty has declined since the 1950s.' (1)

Check yourself

Explanations of poverty

1 Explain what Lewis means by a culture of poverty and why Coates and Silburn reject his view. (2)

2 Write a paragraph about the underclass using the following terms and phrases (in any order): delinquency; unemployment; Murray; over-generous welfare benefits. (4)

3 Read the following statements (**A** and **B**) and identify whether they are victim-blaming or system-blaming explanations.

- **A** 'Recent increases in poverty have been linked to the decline in manufacturing and substantial job losses.' (1)
- **B** 'The poor are individuals who have lost the ability to be self-reliant.' (1)

4 Explain why Dean and Taylor-Gooby describe benefit claimants as 'reluctant dependents'. (1)

5 True or false? 'Weber's ideas provide an explanation of poverty based on class, status and power.' (1)

6 Suggest three reasons why women are over-represented among the poor. (3)

7 Suggest three ways in which poverty serves the capitalist system. (3)

The answers are on pages 116–17.

Welfare

Welfare involves providing for people's needs or **well-being**. It usually refers to meeting 'basic' needs such as housing, healthcare and sufficient income for essentials. Welfare providers may be:

- **Public** The state, for example, provides healthcare through the NHS, paid for through taxation and national insurance contributions.
- **Private** Private, profit-making **companies** provide healthcare, education and other welfare services at a price.
- **Voluntary** Charities such as Shelter and Age Concern use public donations and sometimes government grants to provide services.
- **Informal** Family, friends and neighbours provide services for one another, e.g. caring for an elderly relative.

The aims of the Welfare State are set out in the **1942 Beveridge Report**, which introduced a state system of social insurance to vanquish the 'five giant evils' of **want** (poverty); **idleness** (unemployment); **squalor** (bad housing); **disease** (poor health) and **ignorance** (lack of education).

For 30 years after the Beveridge Report there was '**welfare consensus**'. Most politicians agreed that the welfare state was desirable. However, some on the left argued that welfare policies were not going far enough in addressing poverty and inequality. Others on the right argued that provision such as unemployment benefit encouraged idleness. These differences of view became more pronounced from the mid-1970s.

The political left favours **universal** benefits available to all, rather than means-tested benefits available only to the poor, and argues that welfare should be **institutional** (i.e. all welfare should be provided by the state and not privately). Supporters of this system argue it is fairer and does not stigmatize the poor by making them stand out, it avoids the creation of a poverty trap and administration costs are relatively low.

The political right favours **selective** benefits targeted at those who really need them. The role of the state is seen as **residual** – kept to a minimum – and government should actively encourage the growth of private provision. Supporters argue this is more efficient because it targets those in need while reducing the burden of dependency on the state.

The main **perspectives on the Welfare State** are social democratic, New Right, Marxist and feminist. Each perspective reflects a political position.

- **Social democrats** believe that welfare provision can reduce inequality and promote social integration. They advocate a **strategy of equality**: a gradual process of social reform through expansion of the Welfare State and citizen rights, guaranteeing the right to work, housing, health care and education. **Tawney** believed the welfare state should be a Robin Hood, redistributing wealth from the rich to the poor. This type of thinking greatly influenced the founding of the Labour Party.

  However, Le Grand's evidence suggests that the Welfare State has in fact had little effect on the distribution of income and wealth. All social classes have benefited from the Welfare State so its impact on inequality is minimal. In some areas, such as spending on education, the middle class benefit most. **Westergaard and Resler's research** shows that tax and welfare provision redistributes income and wealth horizontally, i.e. within but not between social classes.

- **New Right** views on welfare and the state became influential during the period of Conservative government from 1979 to 1997. In this view, state involvement in the economy and welfare should be minimal because free enterprise and **market forces** are seen as a more efficient way to provide welfare. The New Right believe in reducing taxation and government spending on welfare so that consumers keep more of their own money and decide how to spend it to meet their own welfare needs. The family rather than the state should have responsibility for welfare. The New Right encourage private provision in areas such as healthcare and pensions. The New Right argue that reduced welfare spending will allow tax cuts and that these will stimulate entrepreneurs (business people) to invest and expand. This will create more wealth overall, some of which will 'trickle down' to the poor.

Critics argue that this '**strategy of inequality**' under Mrs Thatcher in the UK and President Reagan in the USA left the poorer groups **worse** off and **widened** the gap between rich and poor. Critics also claim that increased private provision of welfare leads to a 'two-tier' system in which those who can afford to 'go private' get better services, while the poor are left with inferior, under-funded state provision.

- **Marxists** argue that social equality is impossible in a capitalist society based on the exploitation of one class by another. For Marxists the state – including the welfare state – defends the interests of the ruling class. Workers can, at times, exert pressure to improve welfare benefits, but the gains they make tend to be reversed during periods of economic crisis when the government makes cuts in welfare spending. For Marxists, social equality is not achieved through gradual reform but by the overthrow of capitalism. Marxists are equivocal about the welfare state. On the one hand, welfare benefits have been gained as a result of struggle and must be defended. On the other hand, **the welfare state reproduces and legitimizes capitalism**; for example, the education system and health service reproduce the kind of workforce capitalism requires and the state makes capitalism seem more acceptable to the masses by spending money on welfare services.
- **Feminists** argue that the concept of women's **dependency** is a key to understanding how the welfare state operates and how it oppresses women. **McIntosh** points out that state benefits are based on the assumption that a woman who is cohabiting should be supported by the man she lives with: her husband or partner.

Another example, highlighted by **Land**, is the assumption that women, and not men or the state, are responsible for the care of family members. Feminists are against policies like these, which reinforce **patriarchy**, and campaign in favour of policies that improve women's position, such as equal pay and state-funded childcare.

In recent years there has been a trend towards **welfare pluralism** where the private, voluntary and informal sector provide welfare alongside state provision. Private provision has expanded, including hospitals, schools, health insurance, pensions, residential homes and agencies that supply nursing and care staff.

Another important development is the trend towards **community care** as an alternative to institutional care (i.e. care in institutions such as hospitals and asylums). Community care has been criticized for being driven by a wish to cut costs. **Scull** argues that with the closure of asylums, many ex-inmates have become neglected drifters living rough who receive no care in the community. Gittins points out that because community care has been under-funded, it has shifted responsibility for care of the sick and elderly onto women in the home.

The above developments can be seen as part of a growing **crisis in the welfare state**. Governments have found it increasingly difficult to provide universal benefits and in practice have taken what **Alcock** describes as a **casualty approach** to poverty and other social problems. Thus, for example, welfare provision deals with the extremes of poverty, largely via means-tested benefits, but fails to tackle its structural causes or to reduce inequality overall.

George and Miller detect the beginnings of a new consensus: **the 'affordable welfare state'**. They argue that all the main political parties are now committed to a largely privately owned economy, low rates of income tax and the view that any further improvements in the welfare state must be paid for by improved economic performance.

Check yourself

Wealth, poverty and welfare

Welfare

1 Name the 'five giant evils' identified by Beveridge. (5)

2 True or false? 'A system based on means-tested benefits makes services such as free healthcare and education available to everyone irrespective of income level and need.' (1)

3 Read the following statements (**A–C**) about the welfare state and identify the perspective associated with them.

   A 'Individuals and families should provide for their own needs, not the state.' (1)

   B 'Most welfare policies assume that women are, or should be, economically dependent on men.' (1)

   C 'The welfare state can, and should, bring about social equality through a gradual process of reform.' (1)

4 Explain what is meant by welfare pluralism. (1)

5 Identify two criticisms of community care. (2)

6 Explain what George and Miller mean by 'the affordable welfare state'. (1)

The answers are on page 117.

The management and control of work

Sociologists are interested in the **division of labour**, how it works and who benefits from it.

Weber argued that **bureaucracy** is the most efficient type of organization. A bureaucracy is based on a hierarchy of positions that differ in seniority. A person's position is not determined by nepotism – who you know – but by experience, ability and qualifications. Decision-making is based on impersonal rules and regulations.

Burns and Stalker challenge Weber's view that bureaucracy is always the most efficient form of organization. They distinguish between mechanistic and organic organizations. The latter are less hierarchical and can adapt more quickly to change. **Merton** argues that bureaucracy can lead to mindless rule-following.

Like Weber, **Taylor** was interested in how to improve efficiency and maximize output. He introduced 'time and motion' studies, financial incentives and the selection and training of workers. His approach – known as **Scientific Management** – was widely adopted in the manufacturing industry, e.g. in the assembly-line production of the Model T Ford.

The **Human Relations school** criticizes Scientific Management for ignoring informal work groups. **Mayo's research** at the Hawthorne electrical plant showed that workers are motivated by a need for social approval as well as financial incentives. Productivity is affected by workers' loyalties to the company and to each other.

Marxists such as **Braverman** argue that Scientific Management is geared to maximizing profits for employers through exploitation of the workforce. **Mass production and new technology have deskilled the workforce** by turning previously skilled jobs into a set of repetitive tasks. Taylor's techniques have made production more profitable at the expense of the workforce.

Braverman's critics argue that technological change has resulted in upskilling and not deskilling of the workforce. Views differ about whether automation and information technology cause deskilling or upskilling. **Gallie's research** points to **upskilling** linked to the expansion of **information technology** in the 1980s and 1990s. However, information technology has a differential impact on the workforce. Workers whose jobs are part-time, semi-skilled or unskilled benefit least.

Some argue that work and employment are being transformed, not only by **new technology**, but also by **globalization** and **new production methods**.

Grint includes the following key features in his description of globalization:

- compression of time and space
- 24-hour world financial markets: money never sleeps
- trade dominated by multi-national corporations
- global production methods
- increased competition for global markets
- the spread of the Internet.

Arguably a trend towards globalization is accompanied by a shift from Fordist to Post-Fordist production methods:

- **Fordist production** is based on mass production (e.g. car assembly) and aimed at mass markets. Mass production is highly organized and broken down into component parts with a sharp division between mental and manual work.

- **Post-Fordist production** is specialized and aimed at niche markets. There is centralized control, but decentralized production and subcontracting. More decision-making is delegated to the workforce and there is closer integration of manual and mental work, e.g. through the use of information technology.

Optimists see the above changes as giving employees more control and improving work satisfaction by delegating responsibility and giving scope for creativity. **Pessimists** argue that change has benefited managers and professionals, but not semi- and unskilled workers.

Grint warns against exaggerating the extent of change. Mass production continues to be the main method of producing goods and services, while new post-Fordist production methods have developed on the sidelines. **Callinicos** adds that globally there are more people working in mass production than ever before. From a Marxist perspective he argues that global competition has worsened the position of many working class people.

Alienation and work satisfaction

Marx argued that workers would remain alienated as long as capitalism survived. Workers lack control of capitalist production and do not own the product of their labour. From a Marxist perspective, **alienation** and industrial conflict are inevitable in a society divided into two opposing classes: the bourgeoisie (capitalists) and proletariat (workers).

Blauner argues, however, that the main cause of alienation is mass production technology. He identifies four dimensions of alienation:

- **powerlessness**: lack of control
- **meaninglessness**: lack of purpose
- **isolation**: lack of social relationships
- **self-estrangement**: lack of personal fulfilment.

Blauner's inverted U-curve sums up his view (see below).

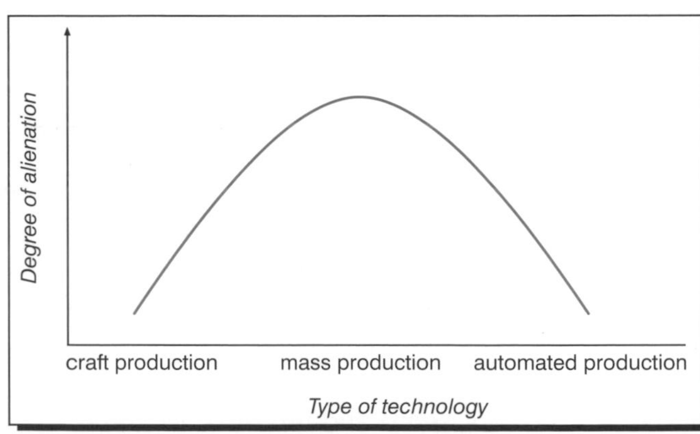

Blauner's 'inverted U curve' (based on Blauner, 1964)

He suggests that alienation reaches a peak with mass production but then decreases, because **automation** creates jobs with more scope for decision-making and self-expression.

Others see **workers' orientations** or attitudes to work as the key determinant of work satisfaction. **Goldthorpe and Lockwood** found that car assembly line workers adopted a calculative and instrumental attitude to work and did not expect to gain satisfaction from it. Gallie's research on oil refinery workers in Britain and France shows that attitudes to work can differ even when the technology is the same, thus contradicting Blauner's view that technology is the key factor. French workers were more militant, reflecting a different political culture.

From a Marxist perspective, **Salaman** argues that alienation stems from the way work is designed and controlled. Like Braverman, he argues that alienation is not inevitable but a result of **capitalist exploitation**. The relationship between exploiter and exploited is something Blauner ignores.

Scase observes that jobs in factories are being replaced by equally alienating and low-paid jobs in service industries. He therefore questions whether fundamental changes predicted by Blauner have taken place. Workers are now supervised in subtler ways, for example, with the use of electronic **surveillance** to monitor work in **call-centres**. The use made of new technology is governed by power relationships in society that have not fundamentally changed.

Postmodernists argue that paid employment is not the only source of social identity and that social class is not the only source of social differences. **Jameson** suggests that schizophrenia, not alienation, is commonly experienced in post-modern society. Instead of being based on a shared experience of exploitation at work, **identity becomes fragmented** and shaped by a range of experiences both within and outside paid employment.

Conflict at work

Sociologists are interested in the causes of strikes and in how conflict at work is also expressed in other ways, for example, though absenteeism or sabotage.

Strikes can be understood either as a temporary breakdown in communication or a symptom of underlying class conflict.

Functionalists believe that society is based on **consensus** and see strikes either as resulting from a breakdown in communication or from the activities of a deviant minority. **Marxists**, however, argue that **conflict** is never far from the surface in a capitalist society where production is based on class exploitation. Developing this point, **Lane and Roberts** conclude that strikes are not extraordinary events but 'perfectly normal events, conducted by perfectly normal people in perfectly normal circumstances'.

The incidence of strikes declined dramatically after the miners' dispute in 1984–5 as the graph below shows.

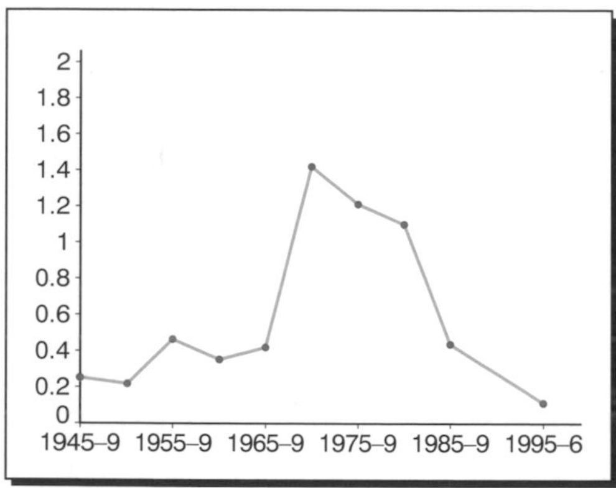

UK strikes, 1945–1996: number of days lost (ten millions)

The following reasons have been put forward:

- legal changes that curbed official and unofficial strike action
- rising unemployment and casualization of work
- distancing of the trade unions by the government
- management of public opinion about 'strike prone' Britain

- privatization of state industries and services
- government controls on public sector pay.

Hyman argues that **government policies** introduced by Mrs Thatcher in the 1980s were the major cause of a reduction in strikes. However, Grint suggests **new technology** and **economic restructuring** had more influence than government policy.

There are several **other types of conflict at work**:

- **Absenteeism and labour-turnover** Rates tend to be high in jobs where workers are dissatisfied or disillusioned.
- **Joking, cursing and intimidatory humour** These can express hostility towards employers and working conditions but reinforce solidarity with workmates.
- **Cheating, fiddling and pilfering** As **Mars and Ditton** both show, such activities can either express group loyalty or be a way to 'get one over' on the employer or customers.
- **Harassment** Problems of harassment and bullying, e.g. of employees by their supervisors or other colleagues.
- **Industrial sabotage** This includes both deliberate vandalism and passive neglect resulting in damage to the employer's property.

Taylor and Walton argue that although sabotage seems senseless to the outside observer, it means something to those involved. Like some of the other examples, it can also be seen as an expression of class conflict. However, the problem of **harassment and bullying** needs to be seen in relation to a broader range of inequalities, including gender and ethnicity.

Check yourself

Work and leisure

The management and control of work

1. True or false? 'Weber believed bureaucracy creates inefficiency.' (1)
2. Write a detailed explanation of what Taylor meant by scientific management. (4)
3. Explain why Taylor's ideas are criticized by the Human Relations school. (1)
4. Which sociologist conducted research at the Hawthorne electrical plant? (1)
5. Write a paragraph about deskilling using as many of the following terms as possible (in any order): deskilling; upskilling; mass production; information technology. (4)
6. Identify three key features of globalization. (3)
7. Suggest two ways in which Fordist production and post-Fordist production differ. (2)

Alienation and work satisfaction

1. Name Blauner's four dimensions of alienation. (4)
2. Write a paragraph about Blauner's explanation of alienation using as many of the following terms as you can (in any order): inverted U curve; automation; mass production; decision-making. (4)
3. What do Goldthorpe and Lockwood identify as the key factor that affects work satisfaction? (1)
4. What reason does Gallie give to explain the greater militancy of French workers as compared with British workers? (1)
5. True or false? 'Postmodernists argue that paid employment is not the only source of identity in today's society.' (1)

Check yourself

Conflict at work

1 Read the following statements (**A** and **B**) about strikes and identify the perspective associated with each:

A 'Strikes are inevitable as long as there is class exploitation.' (1)

B 'Strikes are caused by a breakdown in communication.' (1)

2 Who described strikes as 'perfectly normal events'? (1)

3 Suggest three reasons why the incidence of strikes has declined. (3)

4 Identity four types of conflict at work other than strikes. (4)

The answers are on pages 118–19.

Unemployment

The New Right see the unemployed as part of an underclass or **dependency culture** created by the welfare benefits system; others see unemployment as a **structural problem** caused by economic restructuring (e.g. industrial decline) and government policy.

The **distribution of unemployment** reflects not only the availability of jobs but also the extent to which different social groups face discrimination. This helps to explain why there is a disproportionate number of women, ethnic minorities, older people and the disabled among the unemployed.

Unemployment is defined and measured in different ways:

- The 'headline' figure of unemployment is published monthly and widely reported in the media. This expresses the 'claimant count unemployed' based on the number of people eligible to claim unemployment benefit as a percentage of the workforce.
- The International Labour Office (ILO) defines the unemployed as those without paid employment who are available to start work within a fortnight.
- The Unemployment Unit's definition of the unemployed includes those who have not sought work, including, for example, full-time housewives.

Unemployment statistics must be viewed with caution, because they may underestimate the true extent of unemployment by not classifying certain groups and individuals as 'unemployed', and secondly, by failing to recognize some types of work, either legal or illegal.

The headline figure of unemployment only includes people who are eligible for benefit. Critics argue that this greatly underestimates the true extent of unemployment because many – for example, those on training schemes – can't find work and consider themselves to be unemployed.

Deem comments on the absurdity of classifying women with unpaid domestic responsibilities as 'economically inactive'. Other kinds of work overlooked in official definitions of unemployment are 'moonlighting' or the 'informal economy', i.e. work that is not reported to the Inland Revenue. It is also difficult to measure the extent of illegal work such as prostitution or crime.

The social effects of unemployment can be explained in quantitative and qualitative terms. Studies have examined the facts of unemployment, such as its effects on health, and the experience of unemployment, such as feelings of **social exclusion**.

Pahl's research on the **effects of unemployment on households** found that male unemployment did not lead to role-reversal. Wives who worked full-time continued to be responsible for domestic work and childcare even when their husbands were unemployed.

Grint observes how unemployment destroys the structures of time, routine, social status and social networks associated with work. Thus, although the unemployed have more time to spend on household budgeting or leisure pursuits, in practice they often lose interest and withdraw.

Unemployment has negative effects on **physical and mental health**. The unemployed experience higher rates of all causes of illness, including depression.

Studies show that unemployment brings **loss of identity and self-esteem**. For example, **Allatt and Yeandle** describe the sickness and depression felt by the young unemployed in north-east England who withdrew from their families and social life, often staying in bed all morning. Poverty and lack of status prevented them from gaining independence and making the important step into adulthood.

Leisure

Parker's research examines the relationship between **leisure and occupation**. He sees paid employment (i.e. production) as the main influence shaping individual and group identity. Parker identifies three relationships between occupations and leisure patterns:

- **Opposition pattern** There is a sharp distinction between work and leisure. Leisure compensates for alienation at work, e.g. coal-miners; distant water fishermen; assembly line workers.
- **Extension pattern** There is no sharp distinction between work and leisure because work is 'a central life interest' which offers job satisfaction, e.g. professionals.
- **Neutrality pattern** Work is neither damaging nor fulfilling, but leisure offers a change from work and opportunity for relaxation, e.g. bank clerks.

Roberts argues against the view that occupation is the sole determinant of leisure patterns. He suggests that leisure patterns are also influenced by factors such as age, gender, family cycle and individual choice.

Feminists criticize both Parker and Roberts for **malestream bias** in ignoring the way unpaid domestic work affects women's leisure patterns. From a feminist perspective, both Deem and **Stanley** argue that patriarchy shapes leisure patterns. For example, women's leisure is restricted in the following ways:

- They are discouraged from participating because venues are often male-dominated, e.g. pubs; sports venues.
- They are more restricted financially.
- Their mobility is restricted due to lack of access to transport and fear of street crime.
- Their time is dominated by domestic activities in the home.
- Cultural definitions of femininity restrict their options in leisure.

The fact that women are mainly responsible for **housework and childcare** also frees men to enjoy leisure.

Marxists see leisure as both a source of profit and a form of social control. **Clarke and Critcher** use the concept of hegemony to describe how ruling groups have attempted to 'gentle the masses'. In the 19th century this meant an emphasis on **rational recreation** as a means of 'taming the workforce', and in the 20th century it meant a massive expansion of the leisure industry and the growth of **consumer capitalism**, especially from the 1950s.

Postmodernists put forward a different view. They argue that in post-modern society our social identities are influenced increasingly by patterns of consumption rather than patterns of employment and production. Work is no longer the main influence. The **shift from production to consumption**, coupled with increasing social diversity, results in an almost infinite number of leisure patterns and styles. Individuals and groups construct their own identities through the choices they make about leisure.

Against the postmodernist view, Scase argues that occupation remains central to an understanding of personal identity, lifestyle and social structure. A person's occupation continues to be the main influence on their lifestyle and patterns of consumption because their position in the labour market determines their **access to leisure opportunities and resources**.

Check yourself

Work and leisure

Unemployment

1 Suggest four social groups who may experience relatively high rates of unemployment because of discrimination. (4)

2 Identify three different definitions of unemployment. (3)

3 Identify three kinds of work undertaken by some people that may make official unemployment statistics invalid. (3)

4 True or false? 'Pahl found evidence of role-reversal amongst couples where the husband was unemployed.' (1)

5 What did Allatt and Yeandle find out about the effects of unemployment on young people? (1)

Leisure

1 Read the following statements (**A** and **B**) and say whether they describe an opposition, extension or neutrality pattern of leisure.

A 'A sharp distinction between work and leisure.' (1)

B 'A continuity between work and leisure.' (1)

2 Identify the four factors, apart from work, that Roberts sees as shaping leisure patterns. (4)

3 Suggest three reasons why women's leisure is more restricted than men's. (3)

4 Write a short paragraph on Clarke and Critcher's study using the following terms (in any order): rational recreation; consumer capitalism; hegemony. (3)

5 True or false? 'Postmodernists believe that social identities are influenced increasingly by patterns of consumption rather than patterns of employment.' (1)

6 Explain why Scase believes that occupation remains central to an understanding of personal identity. (1)

The answers are on pages 119–20.

Types and sources of data

Sociologists use a variety of types and sources of data or evidence to test their theories and explanations. **Quantitative data** is information presented in numerical form, e.g. graphs or statistical tables. **Qualitative data** is descriptive rather than numerical and is usually expressed in words to convey feelings and experiences. Quantitative sources include questionnaires, formal interviews and the use of official statistics. Qualitative sources include in-depth interviews, participant observation and the use of diaries.

Primary data is information collected by sociologists themselves for their own sociological purposes, e.g. to test a hypothesis. **Secondary data** is not collected by sociologists themselves, but by others such as governments, charities or individuals who keep personal diaries. Secondary data is usually collected for non-sociological purposes, e.g. governments collect statistics on education or crime to help with policy-making. Sociologists make extensive use of secondary data, often combining it with data from primary sources.

Sociologists use the following criteria when choosing methods and evaluating research findings:

- **Validity** Will the method measure what it sets out to measure, i.e. will it give a true picture?
- **Reliability** Will the findings of the study be replicable, i.e. will they be the same if the study is repeated?
- **Representativeness** Will the sampling method be representative of the wider population to allow generalizations to be made from the findings?
- **Practical considerations** How do factors such as time and money affect the type of method we can use?
- **Subject matter** Will the chosen method be appropriate to the kind of people or activity being studied?
- **Ethical issues** Will the study adhere to ethical guidelines? How will participants in the study give 'informed consent'?

- **Theoretical perspective** The sociologist's preferred perspective may affect the choice of method, e.g. positivists may prefer quantitative methods while interactionists prefer qualitative methods.

Experiments

Contrasts are often drawn between research in the social sciences, including sociology, and experimental research in the **natural sciences**, such as physics and chemistry. Natural sciences make extensive use of laboratory experiments to establish cause and effect relationships between factors or 'variables'. **Experiments** are carried out under controlled conditions to make sure that results are objective and not influenced by the presence of the researcher.

Laboratory experiments are seldom used in sociology. Most sociological research is carried out in society 'as it is' and not in the artificial surroundings of a laboratory. Society is too large and complex to investigate in laboratory conditions and there are ethical objections to experiments on people.

Instead of laboratory experiments, some sociologists use the **comparative method** to identify key variables by comparing 'naturally occurring differences'. An example is Durkheim's study of suicide, which identifies the key variable of 'social integration' by comparing suicide rates in Protestant and Catholic areas. Sociologists also occasionally use **field experiments**, which are conducted in a natural setting rather than a laboratory, but this means it is usually impossible to control all the variables in the situation.

Survey methods

Surveys involve asking people questions. Survey research makes use of questionnaires and interviews to obtain information about a sample of the population. Research begins with the **choice of a topic** to investigate and with **formulating an aim or hypothesis**. A hypothesis is an untested theory, usually expressed as a statement to be proved or disproved.

The next step is usually to conduct a **pilot study**, i.e. a trial-run, which allows potential problems to be identified and adjustments to be made before the survey begins.

Questions may be either closed-ended or open-ended. **Closed-ended questions** give the respondent a fixed list of possible answers to choose from (e.g. Yes/No/Don't know). **Open-ended questions** allow respondents to answer freely in their own words (e.g. 'What made you decide to leave school at 16?').

Surveys make use of a variety of **sampling techniques**, because it is not normally possible to include everyone from the population in a survey. Sampling techniques allow a smaller group of people – a sample – to be selected from the population. The sample is chosen from a **sampling frame**, which is a list of people in a given population, such as the electoral roll or a list of patients at a doctor's surgery. The main types of sampling techniques are as follows:

- **Random sampling** This is where the sample is chosen from the sampling frame literally 'at random' (i.e. by chance) to ensure that it is representative of the survey population.
- **Stratified random sampling** This is where separate random samples are chosen from sub-groups within the survey population, for example, men and women and/or different age groups. This can make it more representative.
- **Quota sampling** This is where an interviewer is not told exactly who to interview but must find a certain number or quota of interviewees who fall into certain categories, e.g. 20 women aged 16–25.
- **Snowball sampling** The researcher builds up a sample by asking respondents to refer him or her to others. This has been used, for example, to study drug-taking. It is usually less representative.

Accurate sampling and a high **response rate** will ensure that a study's findings are representative. A survey's conclusions can be undermined by a low response rate, therefore successful use of follow-up questionnaires or interviews can be important.

Surveys are based on 'asking questions' involving the use of self-completed questionnaires (including postal questionnaires) and structured, semi-structured or unstructured interviews:

- **Questionnaires** These are a relatively cheap and quick way to collect information from a large sample. They can be sent by post or completed on the spot, for example, in a classroom or office. The questions and answers are usually pre-coded (i.e. tick box) and results easily quantified (i.e. turned into statistics).

  Supporters of this method claim the data collected is reliable, easy to quantify and to apply, for instance, when testing a hypothesis and identifying trends. Questionnaires can reach **huge numbers of people**. All respondents answer the same set of questions and they are not influenced by the presence of an interviewer.

  Critics point to the **low response rate** to postal questionnaires. (For example, the Hite Report had a response rate of less than 5 per cent.) Non-response can undermine the representativeness of a sample and, even when the questionnaires are returned, they may not be completed properly. Interactionists argue that by drawing up questions in advance, the researchers prevent respondents from expressing their true feelings, because the researchers have already decided which topics are important. This undermines the validity of the findings.

- **Structured or formal interviews** overcome some of the above problems but offer less scope for surveying large numbers. Structured interviews also use pre-coded questions and answers, but a **trained interviewer** is present to read out the questions and complete the interview schedule. Formal interviews are conducted face-to-face with respondents but they are standardized (i.e. all conducted in the same way) to ensure reliability. They make fairly **efficient use of time and resources**.

  Critics argue that formal interviews lack validity because they give little scope for respondents to express their true feelings. Labov shows that respondents who are reticent in a formal interview can be forthcoming and imaginative when the interview is informal.

- **Semi-structured interviews** give more scope to the interviewer and respondent. An interview schedule is drawn up in advance but some of the questions are likely to be open-ended; they may be asked in any order and different topics may be explored. Dean and Taylor-Gooby approached their interviews with benefit claimants in this way.
- **An unstructured interview** is a 'guided conversation' where the interviewer has complete freedom to decide what questions to ask, and how to ask them. Questions are not pre-determined and are usually open-ended, allowing the respondent to expand in his or her own way.

Supporters of semi- and unstructured interviews argue that they allow the interviewer more freedom and flexibility to explore ideas and develop a hypothesis when conducting research. Semi- and unstructured interviews are more flexible because the situation is not standardized and controlled. It follows, therefore, that more will be revealed about a respondent's true feelings, beliefs and behaviour, so the data is likely to be more valid. Unstructured interviews can achieve greater **empathy** with the respondent because the interviewer has more scope to understand respondents and see things from their point of view.

Critics argue that unstructured interviews lack reliability because no two interviews will be alike. Unstructured interviews are time-consuming, so the sample is likely to be small, making it **harder to generalize** about the findings, i.e. it is difficult to apply the findings to the whole population. Interviewers also need lengthy training to acquire the necessary skills and knowledge of sociology.

Although semi- and unstructured interviews are widely used, they attract theoretical criticism both from positivists, who see them as **lacking reliability**, and from interactionists, who argue that even unstructured interviews create an **artificial situation** and don't go far enough towards studying people in their 'natural' surroundings.

Both structured and unstructured interviews are criticized for the **interviewer effect**: the fact that respondents adjust to the person asking the questions, e.g. giving answers that they think the interviewer wants to hear. The interviewer effect stems from the fact that **interviews are social processes**: they involve interaction between the interviewer and respondent, which inevitably distorts the information obtained.

The above raises the problem of validity because the answers given to questions can be greatly influenced by **the way the respondent perceives the interviewer**. Thus an interviewer of a different gender, class or cultural background is likely to be given different answers to the same questions, for example, **Williams** found African Americans responded differently to black and white interviewers.

Graham argues that surveys often fail to produce valid explanations of women's lives and experiences. Formal methods remove women from the real life situations in which they experience gender inequality. The interview situation prevents respondents from expressing feelings of frustration and antagonism so the true extent of gender inequality remains hidden.

Positivists argue that better training and refinement of the techniques can help to overcome the above difficulties, but many **interactionists** reject interview techniques in favour of an approach based on direct observation.

Check yourself

Sociological methods

Types and sources of data/Experiments

1 Give three examples of quantitative sources of data. (3)

2 Explain the difference between primary and secondary data. (2)

3 List seven criteria sociologists use when they select a research method. (7)

4 Suggest three reasons why laboratory experiments are seldom used in sociology. (3)

Survey methods

1 Explain why pilot studies are used. (1)

2 What is quota sampling? (1)

3 Explain why follow-up questionnaires or interviews are important. (1)

4 Suggest two reasons why questionnaires are considered to be a reliable method. (2)

5 True or false? 'Structured interviews are like a guided conversation.' (1)

6 Suggest three potential weaknesses of postal questionnaires. (3)

7 What type of interviews did Dean and Taylor-Gooby use in their study of benefit claimants? (1)

8 Explain why unstructured interviews are criticized for being unreliable. (1)

9 True or false? 'Unstructured interviews restrict the scope for empathy between interviewer and respondent.' (1)

10 Explain what is meant by the interviewer effect and give an example. (2)

The answers are on pages 120–21.

Observational methods

An alternative to asking people questions is to observe them directly. The main observation method used by sociologists is **participant observation (PO)**, which involves the researcher joining in with the group that he or she wishes to observe. The researcher will often enter the group with an open mind and allow the hypothesis to emerge from the research. Pryce adopted this approach in his study 'Endless Pressure'.

The aim of PO is to gain **understanding** or insight into the lives of the subjects of the study. Its supporters claim PO produces **uniquely valid data** because the best way to gain **insight** into other people's lives and experiences is through personal involvement.

When conducting **overt** PO the researcher does not disguise his or her identity, but with **covert** PO the researcher conceals their true identity and purpose, literally going 'under-cover', usually by pretending to be one of the group.

Covert PO can give access to aspects of social life that are secret or deviant but critics object on the following grounds:

- **Practical problems** Routine aspects of conducting the study are likely to raise suspicion, such as asking questions and taking notes. Covert observers run the risk of their cover being blown, and possibly personal injury.
- **Ethical problems** Covert PO involves the researcher getting information by deception and contravening the principle of 'informed consent', i.e. that subjects should be told what a study is about and agree to take part.

  Humphreys is criticized for disregarding ethics, not only because his observation was covert, but also because he noted the car registration numbers of the homosexuals he observed so that he could trace and interview them later.

PO can be divided into three stages:

- **Getting in** Initially the observer will contact the group and work at gaining their trust. This may mean establishing a relationship with a key informant as a first step to gaining access to the group. For example, in **Whyte's study** of 'Street Corner Society', his key informant was the leader, Doc. Some groups are easier to join than others. This will depend, in part, on the characteristics of the researcher and the group. Differences of age, class, gender or ethnicity can be an obstacle. The researcher also needs to decide what role to adopt.
- **Staying in** The researcher has to strike a balance between being an observer and being a participant. The researcher needs to remain detached to study the group sociologically. However, he or she also needs to become involved with the group to understand them. There is a danger of the observer's objectivity being undermined by '**going native**', by being too involved with the group and seeing things only from their point of view. Whyte notes that he began as a non-participant observer but ended up as a non-observing participant.
- **Getting out** This presents further challenges, especially with covert PO. It may be difficult for the sociologist to explain why he or she is **leaving the group** and to break the emotional attachments formed during the study. Whyte reports that he had difficulty re-adjusting to life when his research ended.

PO has been widely used for the study of crime and deviance where suspicion of outsiders makes the use of survey methods impractical. As **Yablonski** points out, deviant groups are distrustful of researchers who want answers to questions. An advantage, therefore, is that PO provides evidence that could not be gathered by other methods. Evidence gathered by direct observation does not rely on respondents' answers to questions. Since observations are conducted in **natural settings** it is also less likely that researchers will impose their versions of reality on the people being studied.

However, PO is usually **small-scale** research, and the samples are not usually chosen systematically. The group included in the study may not be typical, so it is difficult to generalize the findings to the wider population. PO also lacks reliability because it is unlikely that another researcher repeating the study would observe the same things or reach the same conclusions.

Secondary sources

Official statistics are a major source of secondary data for sociologists. They provide evidence of social trends, such as changing family patterns, educational achievement and crime rates. They can also be used to test a hypothesis, as in Durkheim's study of suicide.

Official statistics are collected by the state either by registration (e.g. births, marriages, deaths) or by surveys (e.g. the General Household Survey). **Unofficial statistics** are collected by agencies other than the state, such as pressure groups, trade unions, businesses and churches. Unofficial statistics have been used by sociologists, for example, **Wilson** used church attendance statistics in his study of secularization.

The practical advantage of statistics is that they are a free source of **huge quantities of data**. However, there may be omissions: statistics may not be available on a particular topic. Durkheim found in his study of suicide that the victim's religion was not recorded on the death certificate. As a result he had to compare suicide rates in Protestant and Catholic areas. Another drawback is that the definitions that lie behind official statistics may be unsociological, such as the Registrar-General's definition of social class.

Depending on their theoretical perspective, sociologists hold widely different views about the usefulness of official statistics:

- **Positivists** see them as a useful source of data that covers large numbers. The census covers the whole UK population. Positivists believe that, provided they are accurate, official statistics are a reliable and valid source of data.

- **Interactionists** are extremely critical of official statistics. For example, they argue that crime statistics are socially constructed and probably tell us more about the priorities of the police than about patterns of crime. In this view, official statistics are not a valid measure of the nature and distribution of crime. **Atkinson** puts forward this view in his study of coroner's suicide verdicts.
- **Marxists** argue that the state serves the interests of the ruling class and therefore official statistics (published by the state) give a distorted impression that serves capitalism. Definitions of **unemployment** have regularly been changed and almost always with the result that the numbers officially counted as unemployed have been reduced.

Documents are a secondary source of **qualitative** data: usually written texts such as personal diaries, government reports, medical records, novels, newspapers and letters. Documents can also be electronic texts (including the output of the mass media), works of art, music or styles of dress.

The classic example of the use of documents in sociological research is **Thomas and Znaniecki's study** of the Polish peasant in Europe and America, which used 764 letters, biographies and autobiographies and public documents (including newspaper articles, court and social work documents) to explore the experience of Polish migration to the USA in the early 20th century.

However, the sources used by Thomas and Znaniecki are **impressionistic** and there is no way of telling whether they are representative. The data is **open to a variety of interpretations** so it is difficult to tell how close it comes to the truth. The advantage of the method, however, is the **unique insight it gives into events**. Its validity can be checked against primary data collected, for example, by interview.

Content analysis is a way of dealing systematically with documents and is widely used in studies of the mass media. It often involves careful recording of the number of images or references contained in the output of the mass media, such as the number of references made to strikes in television news or the way men and women are portrayed in magazines. An example is 'Bad News', a study carried out by the **Glasgow University Media Group**. Content analysis can be a relatively cheap and effective source of data.

Case studies, longitudinal studies and triangulation

A **case study** is a close examination of a single case or example. Case studies can be based on survey research or observation or any other method and can use primary or secondary sources or both.

The main drawback of case studies is that we cannot always easily generalize about their results because we cannot be sure that a single case is a typical case. However, case studies have practical advantages. Case studies are less expensive than national surveys and, although they are smaller, can nevertheless provide detailed evidence for testing a hypothesis (e.g. Goldthorpe and Lockwood's study of affluent workers) or comparing social groups, processes and events (e.g. Gallie's study comparing British and French oil refinery workers).

A **longitudinal study** is one that follows the same sample or group over an extended period of time. The best examples are surveys such as Douglas' study, which followed all the children born in England and Wales in the same week in 1946 and the **National Child Development Survey** based on a sample born in 1958. Some PO studies are longitudinal, for example, Lacey spent four years studying pupils at Hightown Grammar. The advantage of longitudinal studies is that they trace developments over a period of time, although there can be problems keeping track of the original group.

Triangulation is a technique that involves using more than one kind of method or source when carrying out research, for example, a study might combine observation with informal interviews and also use official statistics. The term 'triangulation' means an approach that looks at something from more than one point of view, but not necessarily three! The aim of triangulation is that the **different methods or sources used** complement each other.

Check yourself

Sociological methods

Observational methods

1 Name a study where the researcher began with an open mind, allowing the hypothesis to emerge. (1)

2 Explain the difference between covert and overt PO. (2)

3 Suggest two practical problems with covert PO. (2)

4 Explain why Humphreys' study has been criticized. (1)

5 Explain what is meant by 'going native'. (1)

6 Identify the three stages of doing participant observation. (3)

7 Write a paragraph about the advantages and disadvantages of PO using the following terms (in any order): natural settings; uniquely valid data; re-test reliability; small scale. (4)

Secondary sources

1 Identify the two main methods used for collecting government statistics. (2)

2 Read the following statements (**A–C**) and identify the perspective associated with each one.

A 'Unemployment statistics are a prime example of how the state manipulates information.' (1)

B 'Crime statistics are socially constructed. They tell us more about police procedures than about criminal behaviour.' (1)

C 'Provided they are accurate, official statistics are a reliable and objective source of data.' (1)

3 True or false? 'Sociologists use newspapers as a source of primary data.' (1)

4 What types of documents did Thomas and Znaniecki use in their study of the Polish peasant in Europe and America? (3)

5 Give an example of a study based on content analysis. (1)

Case studies, longitudinal studies and triangulation

1 True or false? 'Case studies are based on large national samples.' (1)

2 Explain what is meant by a longitudinal study and give two examples. (3)

3 True or false? 'Triangulation is where three different research methods are used in a study.' (1)

The answers are on page 121.

Culture and socialization

Note *This chapter is only applicable for students taking the OCR examination.*

Culture and socialization are key concepts for explaining the relationship between the individual and society. Each sociological perspective sees culture and socialization differently, but what unites them is the view that human behaviour is greatly influenced by the environment. To a large extent, human behaviour is based on **learning** and not **instinct**, and is the product of **nurture** rather than **nature**, environment rather than heredity.

A useful starting point is Parsons' distinction between social structure and social processes. Parsons uses the term **social structure** to describe the norms and values of society, in other words, culture. In this view, social life is possible only because members of society share a common system of values. **Social processes**, which include socialization and social control, are processes that encourage conformity to shared norms and values. The **socialization** process ensures that 'new' members of society internalize the culture, whilst the process of **social control** rewards conformity and punishes deviance.

Parsons' view of culture is similar to that of early anthropologists who saw **culture as a blueprint or design for living**. In this view, culture is the whole way of life of a community: everything that humans learn socially rather than inheriting biologically. **Tylor** defined culture as all the knowledge, beliefs, art, morals, laws, customs and other capabilities and habits acquired by members of a society.

Jencks defines culture as 'the learned aspects of society' and socialization as the process through which individuals acquire a culture. Jencks identifies 'three prominent keynotes' in sociological views of culture:

- **Culture is transmitted**: it is a heritage of social traditions.
- Culture is **learned**: it is not inherited biologically.
- Culture is **shared** by members of a social group.

Agencies of socialization are institutions that transmit norms, values, beliefs, knowledge, attitudes and skills. Foremost among these are the family and school. Parsons distinguishes between **primary socialization** (carried out mainly within the home and family) and **secondary socialization** (carried out by the school and other institutions). Other agencies of socialization include the mass media, churches and the workplace. In fact, all institutions are agencies of socialization to an extent.

Social structure

Social structure is a key sociological term. Durkheim saw social structure as a set of moral constraints acting on individuals and binding them into a single community. Linked to this **functionalist view** of social structure is the view that society is composed of social institutions and social roles.

Social institutions are established patterns of behaviour that range from marriage and the family to political, legal and religious institutions. **Social roles** are positions in social institutions. Taken from drama, the term 'role' describes the parts individuals play in society. Each role has a particular **status**, depending on its position in the social structure. A role consists of a set of norms that define the behaviour expected of the social actor who occupies it. Role expectations and behaviour are learned through the process of socialization.

Functionalism is criticized for putting forward an **over-integrated view** of social structure. **Marxists** point to basic conflicts of interest between 'exploiter and exploited, oppressor and oppressed' and argue that social institutions serve to justify and preserve the power and privilege of the dominant class. Thus capitalism is based on conflict and exploitation and not on shared values and cooperation as functionalists claim.

Interactionists criticize functionalism for seeing human behaviour as determined entirely by the social structure. **Wrong** describes functionalism as an **over-socialized view** that allows little scope for individual differences and free choice. Interactionists focus on the micro-level of small-scale interaction between individuals rather than large-scale social structures as functionalists do. Unlike functionalists, interactionists see socialization as an active process involving **choice and negotiation**, not merely a passive, one-way process of social conditioning.

Interactionists accept that individuals are influenced by society, but also see them as capable of standing back and interpreting the roles they play. **Turner** distinguishes between **taking roles** and **making roles**: we take roles from society but we also interpret and create or make them.

A further contrast with functionalism is that interactionism sees culture as diverse and pluralistic, i.e. many **cultures and subcultures co-exist**, rather than assuming that everyone is socialized into the same culture. Arguably, therefore, interactionism is better equipped than functionalism to explain differences of individual and subcultural identity.

Identity

The term **identity** refers to an individual's sense of self, their subjectivity, who they identify with, and who they think they are. The **process of forming an identity** is a social one. It develops through the process of socialization in social groups. Thus our identities are shaped by our experiences of class, ethnicity, nationality, age, gender, etc. All the main perspectives contribute to an understanding of social identity.

Class identity

Marxists focus on **class identity**. Marx himself distinguished between 'the facts of class', i.e. the actual or objective class conditions, and 'the consciousness of class', i.e. how people see their positions in the class structure. A strong sense of **class consciousness** exists when members of a class recognize their shared economic position.

However, people in the same class position do not necessarily share a common identity, for example, many members of the working class may experience 'false consciousness', perhaps seeing other groups of workers as their enemy, rather than the capitalist class who exploit them. A classic example of false consciousness is the way **racism** has prevented the development of class identity by dividing the working class.

While Marxists attach prime importance to social class, critics argue that gender, ethnicity and other social divisions are equally important.

Gender identity

Oakley distinguishes between **sex** (the biological differences between males and females) and **gender**, which refers to culturally created differences: what society defines as 'masculine' and 'feminine' behaviour, roles, attitudes, expectations, dress, jobs, etc. Rather than being inborn (like sex), gender identity is the result of **gender role socialization**.

Connell's research on masculinity adds another dimension to explanations of gender identity. He shows that there are dominant and subordinate forms of masculinity and femininity. Gay **sexuality**, for example, is a subordinate form of masculinity.

Ethnic identity

Lawson and Garrod define **ethnic groups** as 'people who share common history, customs and identity, as well as, in most cases, language and religion, and who see themselves as a distinct unit'.

National identity and **ethnic identity** are similar terms, but where the former is an expression of political identity linked directly or indirectly to a geographical area, the latter is based on a shared cultural heritage. Thus, for example, you might think of yourself as a member of the Welsh/Australian/Albanian nation and/or as part of the Jewish/African-Caribbean/Punjabi cultural heritage.

The term **ethnicity** highlights a shared cultural identity, but the idea of '**race**' is based on supposed biological differences. There is very little evidence that racial groups exist in any real and objective sense. However, the fact that some people are racist (i.e. they believe in racial differences) means they are likely to discriminate against others on racial grounds. It follows that part of the shared identity of an ethnic group often develops because of **a shared experience of racism and discrimination**, for example, the discrimination experienced in education, employment and housing.

The **postmodernist view** is that society is becoming increasingly diverse and that this is reflected in the **diversity** of individual and group identities. Postmodernists argue that social class is not the only important source of identity as Marxists suggest. They believe other sources of identity are equally significant, including gender and sexuality, ethnicity, nationality, disability, age and religion. They argue that we have **choice** and that this plays a large part in the way we construct our identities. In reply, **Marxists** argue that the extent of an individual's choice is greatly influenced by their **class position**.

Check yourself

The individual and society

Culture and socialization

1 True or false? 'Social behaviour is largely instinctive.' **(1)**

2 Briefly explain what is meant by socialization. **(1)**

3 What are the 'three prominent keynotes' Jencks identifies in sociological views of culture? **(3)**

4 True or false? 'The family is the main agency responsible for secondary socialization.' **(1)**

Social structure

1 Briefly explain what is meant by social role. **(1)**

2 True or false?

A 'Interactionists criticize functionalism for failing to recognize that individuals have choice.' **(1)**

B 'Marxists criticize functionalism for ignoring social conflict and exploitation.' **(1)**

3 Explain what Turner means by the 'taking' and 'making' of social roles. **(2)**

Identity

1 Briefly explain what is meant by identity. **(1)**

2 Write a paragraph about class identity using as many of the following terms as possible (in any order): class consciousness; false consciousness; racism. **(3)**

3 Explain Oakley's distinction between sex and gender. **(2)**

4 Explain the difference between ethnicity and 'race'. **(2)**

5 True or false? 'National identity is an expression of political identity linked directly or indirectly to a geographical area.' **(1)**

6 True or false? 'Where postmodernists see all forms of social diversity as equally important, Marxists argue that social class continues to be the most basic and significant source of social difference and inequality.' **(1)**

The answers are on page 122.

Check yourself answers

FAMILIES AND HOUSEHOLDS (pages 4 and 13)

Perspectives on the family

1 **A** The New Right. (1) Very similar to functionalism in favouring a clear-cut sexual division of labour, but the emphasis on 'self-reliance' is a distinctive feature of New Right views.

B Postmodernism. (1) The key is the idea that people now have greater choice and this produces greater diversity in family arrangements.

C Functionalism. (1) They stress the importance of shared values (a 'value consensus') in holding society together, and of the family in passing these values on.

D Liberal feminism. (1) The phrase 'oppression of women' tells us it's a feminist view. The idea of gradual change indicates that it is liberal feminism.

E Interactionism. (1) A key idea for any interactionist explanation is meanings (or labels, or how we define a situation).

2 They are the primary socialization of the young (1) and the stabilization of adult personalities. (1) Compare this with the functions of the family Murdock identifies.

3 The term 'patriarchy' refers to a system of male domination and female oppression, from which men benefit. (1) This operates in society at large and at the 'micro' level of the family and household.

4 *Radical feminism* believes that *patriarchy* is the main problem faced by women. Men as such are the oppressors of women. Radical feminists generally believe that the family is the root of this oppression. (1) *Marxist feminists* see *capitalism* as the main source of women's oppression. Women's subordinate role in the family benefits capitalists, e.g. by servicing the male labour force free of charge and by providing a reserve army of labour. (1)

The family and industrialization

1 The 'structurally isolated nuclear family' refers to a nuclear family that has no binding ties or obligations to wider kin. (1)

2 Geographical mobility refers to movement from one place to another (e.g. from country to town in search of work). (1) Social mobility refers to movement from one social status to another (e.g. son of peasant farmer becomes teacher). (1) Nuclear families are smaller and more geographically mobile. (1)

3 Stage One: pre-industrial nuclear family; (1) Stage Two: early industrial extended family; (1) Stage Three: symmetrical nuclear family (in modern industrial society). (1)

4 Because, although households might only contain nuclear families, there may be a strong extended family network of relatives living close by but in other households. (1)

Check yourself answers

Roles and relationships within the family

1 'Joint conjugal roles' refers to role relationships between husbands and wives where domestic tasks (housework and childcare) are shared. (1) 'Segregated conjugal roles' involves a sharp division of labour: husband as breadwinner and wife as homemaker, responsible for housework and childcare. (1) With joint roles, leisure time is likely to be shared, but with segregated roles, it is likely to be spent separately.

2 'Symmetrical family' is a term used by Willmott and Young to describe the Stage Three family, in their view the dominant family type in modern industrial society. Conjugal roles are joint and more equal, though not identical. (1) Any two of the following: women working; labour-saving devices in the home; geographical mobility (separating nuclear families from their kin); affluence; having fewer children. (2) Note Oakley's criticisms of Willmott and Young's study.

3 Because her research shows that women still do most of the housework and childcare (even when they also go out to work) and even when men do housework, they only 'help', i.e. it's still seen as the woman's responsibility. (1)

4 The distribution of resources within the marriage; (1) decision-making; (1) domestic violence. (1)

5 'The social construction of childhood' refers to the idea that 'childhood' is not a natural, biological state but a social status. What counts as 'childhood' is defined by society. (1) Note examples of how childhood differs between cultures and periods of history.

6 Child labour laws and compulsory schooling. (2)

Family diversity and changing family patterns

1 Organisational; cultural; social class; life stage; cohort (generational). (5)

2 The New Right, or functionalism. (1)

3 About 40 per cent in each case. (2) Most births outside marriage are to cohabiting couples, not lone mothers.

4 Any two of the following: divorce may create one-person households; lone-parent families; reconstituted (step-) families; cohabiting couples. (2)

Families and social policy

1 Any one of the following ways: generous welfare benefits mean that individuals (especially fathers) don't have to take responsibility for their families by working to provide for them. Men can abandon their families, leaving it to the welfare state and taxpayers to provide. Boys are deprived of role models, children become undisciplined in the absence of a father and juvenile delinquency increases. A culture of dependency on welfare develops. (1)

2 Either of the following: feminists see social policy as controlling women and maintaining their dependence on men; Donzelot sees it as a means of surveillance. (1)

Check yourself answers

Health (pages 20–1 and 28)

Medical and social models of health

1 **A** False. It takes a curative approach to disease. (1) **B** True. (1)

Class inequalities in health and health care

1 Morbidity refers to sickness, (1) whereas mortality means death. (1)

2 Any two of the following: higher death rates from almost all diseases; higher infant mortality and stillbirth rates; higher death rates from accidents; more chronic illness; more disability; worse dental condition; lower birth weight; shorter average height; worse self-perceived health; worse mental health; higher blood pressure. (2)

3 **A** Cultural or behavioural explanation. (1)
B Structural or material explanation. (1)
C Social selection explanation. (1)
D Structural or material explanation. (1)

4 **A** Social selection explanation. (1)
B Cultural or behavioural explanation. (1) System-blaming explanations are an alternative to victim-blaming explanations.

5 The 'inverse care law' states that 'the availability of good medical care varies inversely with the needs of the population served'. (1) What this means is that working class areas, where there is most ill health, get fewer resources, GPs, hospital beds, etc., than middle class areas, where there is least illness.

Gender differences in health and health care

1 Married women (1) and single men. (1)

2 Any two of the following: women may simply be ill more often than men; housewives, not having to go to work, may have time to attend the surgery; as primary carers for children or elderly relatives, women have to visit the doctor anyway and may use this as an opportunity to raise their own health problems; women may be more prepared to discuss problems with doctors; because pregnancy and childbirth are medicalized, most women inevitably come into contact with doctors. (2)

3 Informal care is care provided by non-professionals (family, friends, etc.). (1) Women provide most of it because caring is seen as their primary role in the household division of labour. (1) Most professional care is also provided by women in occupations such as nursing and childcare.

Ethnic differences in health and health care

1 Either of the following: the difficulty of defining an 'ethnic group' (e.g. should all 'whites' be seen as one group, or should Irish and British be regarded as separate ethnic groups?); the health of different groups may also be more to do with their class position than with their ethnicity as such. (1)

Check yourself answers

2 Either of the following: problems of communication, especially for non-English speakers; institutional racism: the NHS has few non-whites in senior positions, and may have an ethnocentric culture. (1) Ethnocentric means bias which stems from looking at something – in this case health care – from the point of view of only one culture.

Medicine and the medical profession

1 'Iatrogenic illness' means illness caused by medical intervention, (1) e.g. prescribing the wrong medication, administering the wrong dose, side effects of medicines, etc. (1)

2 Chronic illness means long-term or permanent (and usually incurable though not immediately life-threatening) illness. (1) Examples include arthritis, asthma and diabetes. (1) Note the difference between *chronic* and *acute* illness.

3 **A** Functionalism. (1)
B Weberians. (1)
C Feminism. (1)

4 Because society grants them high status, on the basis of their technical expertise and scientific knowledge. (1)

5 Rights: exemption from one's normal role obligations (e.g. work, school, domestic duties); the right to be looked after by others. (1) Obligations: to want to get well; to seek competent (i.e. professional medical) help; to obey doctor's orders so as to get well. (1)

6 Any two of the following: social control of the workforce; reproduction/maintenance of the workforce in a fit state to work; an ideological function (masking the exploitative nature of society); providing a source of profits (e.g. for drugs companies). (2)

The social construction of health, illness and disability

1 Any two of the following: because they have a high social status; because they have specialist knowledge; because usually the patient needs them more than they need the patient; because the consultation takes place on their terms (e.g. territory, time, duration). (2)

2 Impairment is a loss of function, whether physical, sensory or intellectual. (1) Disability is a restriction placed on those with impairments by society. (1) Disability is a prime example of a social construct, i.e. something created by society.

Mental illness

1 **(a)** Positivists would argue that the differences are due to differences in the social position or environment of different groups, which exposes them to different pressures and risks. (1) **(b)** Interactionists would see it as a result of some groups being more likely to be labelled as mentally ill. (1)

2 Firstly, women's roles in patriarchal society cause stress, depression, unhappiness, sense of failure (e.g. because unable to achieve an 'ideal' body shape). (1) Secondly, due to labelling/stereotyping of women by the medical profession. (1) The first reason is similar to a positivist explanation; the second is like an interactionist view.

MASS MEDIA (pages 34–5 and 41)

Perspectives on the mass media

1 A Elite theory. (1) The reference to 'brainwashing', 'propaganda' and 'the masses' tells us this is elite theory. Don't confuse elite theory with Marxism; make a note of their similarities and differences.
B Feminism. (1) In this view the output of the mass media transmits patriarchal ideology, i.e. ideas and images which justify men's power over women.
C Postmodernism. (1) The reference to 'media-saturated society' indicates this is a postmodernist view.
D Marxism. (1) Marxists see the media as part of big business and an instrument of ruling class power. The concept of ideology is central to Marxist explanations.

2 False. (1) Pluralists believe that control of the media is ultimately held by consumers whose decisions influence the output of the mass media.

3 True. (1) The reference to 'labelling' points to an interactionist approach.

Ownership, control and output of the mass media

1 Corporate control means control by large business corporations. (1) Corporate control has increased because of mergers and take-overs. (1)

2 Consumer sovereignty means the customer is king. (1) Pluralists believe that power rests with consumers (i.e. audiences) because media companies must attract audiences to stay in business.

3 Marxists reject consumer sovereignty because, in their view, power is held by top executives in media corporations. (1)

4 Instrumentalists see the media as an instrument of ideological control. (1) Structuralists see it as part of big business, greatly influenced by the demands of advertising and finance. (1)

5 Global media are worldwide communications. (1) Interactive media involve two-way communication where the audience takes part. (1) Satellite broadcasting is an example of global media; computer games are interactive media. The Internet is both global and interactive.

Check yourself answers

Selection and presentation of news

1. The Glasgow University Media Group has identified biases in television coverage of strikes. These included the use of *biased vocabulary*, (1) for example, when strikers are described as 'making demands' and employers are portrayed as 'making offers' and trying to be reasonable. Another source of bias is the *selective use of visuals*, (1) for example, a biased impression is given by interviewing employers in the calm surroundings of their offices and workers on a noisy picket line. These examples show that there is a *hierarchy of access* (1) to the mass media with employers given better coverage. These findings support a *Marxist perspective* (1), which sees the media as serving the interests of the ruling class (i.e. employers).
2. According to Galtung and Ruge, dramatic incidents are highlighted in foreign news because of the demands of the 24-hour news cycle and pressure for stories. (1)
3. Deviance amplification is a vicious circle set in motion when the media draws attention to deviant behaviour, exaggerates the problem and prompts a negative reaction from the police and public. (1) Cohen's classic study of Mods and Rockers traces the course of a moral panic.
4. Hall argues that the mass media plays a secondary role in the labelling process because the media relies on information provided by primary definers, such as the police and other official agencies. (1) This can be linked to 'hierarchies of credibility'.
5. Moral panics have been given a new dimension because the media now draw on a wider range of sources, and minority groups usually have experts and self-help groups to represent them. (1)
6. Pastiche refers to images from various different sources that are put together for visual impact. (1) For example, a news report could include computer graphics, archive footage and an interview with someone on the spot. (1)

Representations of social groups in the media

1. Any two of the following: Golding and Middleton's study of 'scroungerphobia'; Glennon and Butsch's study of sitcoms; the Glasgow University Media Group's study of strikes. (2)
2. Jhally and Lewis found that *The Cosby Show* masked the existence of racism. (1) Hartmann and Husband show how news reports contain racial stereotypes. (1)
3. According to Ferguson, representations of women have changed from an emphasis on femininity to an emphasis on self-esteem and mutual support. (1)
4. Connell uses the term 'exemplary masculinity' to describe stereotypes of the ideal man in the media. (1) Gross uses the term 'symbolic annihilation' to describe how the existence of lesbians and gay men is ignored by the media. (1)
5. Two of the main images of old age in the media are dependency (e.g. old age as a second childhood) (1) and images of the young-old enjoying leisure. (1)
6. Cumberbatch and Negrine suggest that disability is invisible in the media, (1) but Darke identifies disability as a central theme in many popular films. (1)

Check yourself answers

The mass media and audience effects

1 True. (1) As the term hypodermic implies, this model sees the content of the media as having a direct effect, as if injected directly into audiences.

2 Any two of the following: the influence of primary groups; the influence of opinion leaders; people make selective use of the media; people's existing attitudes act as a protective net. (2)

3 From a Marxist point of view the scapegoating of minorities deflects attention from class inequality. (1) This is how Marxists explain racism.

4 Hall's model brings together *encoding* (1) (i.e. the way media messages are produced) and *decoding* (1) (i.e. the way audiences interpret the messages). Hall agrees with Althusser that the mass media transmits a *dominant ideology*; (1) however he argues that audiences are capable of *differential de-codings*. (1)

5 Early feminist explanations saw the media as having a direct effect. Women were seen as victims of patriarchal ideology (ideas supporting male power). More recently, feminists have shown that sections of the media play a part in opposing patriarchy. (1)

EDUCATION (pages 52–4 and 58)

Class differences in educational achievement

1 False. (1) The opposite is true. Despite an overall increase in the number of students in higher education, the proportions of students from different class backgrounds has changed very little.

2 Some explanations of class differences in achievement concentrate on the influence of *external factors*, (1) especially the effects of *cultural deprivation*. (1) Seen from a *functionalist perspective*, (1) under-achievement results from a deprived family background that does not provide children with the encouragement or skills they need. Keddie challenges this view. She argues that *cultural deprivation is a myth* (1) that tries to blame working class children for failing in education when really the education system itself is to blame. The theory of cultural deprivation offers a similar explanation of ethnic differences in achievement, and attracts similar criticisms.

3 A self-fulfilling prophecy is a positive or negative label (i.e. a prediction) that affects a child's self-image and causes an improvement or deterioration in the child's achievements. (1)

4 Any two of the following: teachers' negative perceptions; low expectations; streaming; the hidden curriculum; pupil sub-cultures. (2)

5 Any three of the following: the National Curriculum standardized tests; Local Management of Schools; permission for open enrolment; 'opting out' of local authority control; league tables. (3)

6 Parents who are better off and better educated themselves are able to seek out successful schools (1) and can afford travelling expenses. (1) This ties in with Bourdieu's theory of cultural capital.

7 Cream-skimming is where schools try to recruit only highly able pupils. (1) Silt-shifting is where schools try to shift the responsibility for less able pupils elsewhere (i.e. onto other schools). (1)

Ethnic differences in educational achievement

1 Percentages varied from approximately 40 per cent for pupils of Indian origin (1) and 36 per cent for white pupils (1) to 29 per cent for Bangladeshi, (1) 21 per cent for Pakistani (1) and 17 per cent for pupils of African Caribbean origin. (1) It is useful to memorize key statistics for the exam, but be selective: choose a few statistics to illustrate class, gender and ethnic differences in achievement.

2 It is important to distinguish between ethnic minorities because their levels of achievement differ. (1) Failure to distinguish between ethnic groups leads to stereotyping. Different levels of achievement of ethnic groups partly reflect class differences.

3 Pryce suggests the lower achievements of African Caribbean pupils can be traced back to the damaging effects of slavery, but Asian culture, he argues, was not damaged to the same extent. (1)

4 Driver attributes the higher achievements of West Indian girls to the matrifocal (mother-centred) structure of West Indian families. (1) Fuller puts forward a similar explanation for the academic success of the group of black girls in her study.

5 Any one of the following reasons: they ignored Asian customs; they assumed Asian children would have language difficulties; they thought African Caribbean children posed a threat. (1)

6 It restricted their access to teachers' time, unbiased careers advice and learning materials. (1) This study provides evidence of racism and an explanation of its effects.

7 Supporters of ERA believed that the *local management of schools* (1) would give local communities – including ethnic minorities – more control of schools. However, studies do not support this view. Hatcher's research on *school governing bodies* (1) found that they continued to be dominated by *white social networks* (1) whilst Deem found that *decision-making* (1) remained with headteachers and financial experts. Gillborn describes the effect of ERA as *depluralization*; (1) for example, the content of the *National Curriculum* (1) gives little or no recognition to minority cultures and religions.

Gender differences in educational achievement

1 False. (1) Contrary to press reports about 'failing boys', boys' achievements actually improved during the period the gender gap closed.

2 Any two of the following: teachers give more priority to boys; they give the impression that what girls say is less interesting and important; they give girls less attention; girls' self-confidence is undermined. (2) Recent research focuses more on boys and girls' different learning styles.

Check yourself answers

3 Girls' improved achievements were 'against the odds' because they took place against the background of right-wing educational policies and a backlash against feminism. (1)

4 Any four of the following: equal opportunity initiatives; the challenging of stereotypes; encouraging girls to want careers; more appointments of women to senior positions in schools; introduction of GCSE; the National Curriculum; league tables. (4)

5 Any two of the following: fewer women are now full-time housewives; women's employment has increased; arguably the male breadwinner role has been undermined; women's perceptions have been changed by the women's movement. (2)

6 Gender routes are the different pathways boys and girls follow in education. (1) The term can also be used more broadly, e.g. in relation to employment. Sociologists trace gender preferences to early childhood experiences and the way teachers respond to male and female pupils. (1) Gender preferences have become a major theme of research on gender and education.

Perspectives on the role of education in society

1 **A** Functionalist. (1) Durkheim argues that the main function of education is to promote social solidarity by transmitting the values of society to the next generation.

B Functionalist. (1) Parsons sees the American education system as a meritocracy where competition and selection is based on ability and effort. Note the similarities and differences between Durkheim and Parsons' views.

C Postmodernist. (1) In this view, society has become so diverse and fragmented that it is not possible to generalize about how the whole of it works. What we can do is look at how individuals and groups construct their identities and the meaning that education, the family, etc. has for them.

D New Right. (1) These views gained influence in Britain and elsewhere from the 1980s. In this view mass education is inefficient. More power should be delegated to schools and parents should have more influence.

2 Schools reproduce a workforce with the skills needed at different levels of the capitalist economy. (1) They legitimize inequalities by making them seem fair and natural. (1)

3 Education exists 'in the long shadow of work' because it reproduces the workforce the capitalist economy requires. (1) This is what Bowles and Gintis mean by the correspondence principle. Structures in the education system correspond to, and reproduce the authority structures, skills and attitudes that exist in factories, offices, etc.

4 MacDonald criticizes Bowles and Gintis for failing to apply their explanations to gender divisions. (1)

5 Ball argues that the National Curriculum, formula funding and league tables are mechanisms that allow central government to control schools from a distance, thus limiting the influence of parents and local communities. (1) Ball maintains that these mechanisms play an important part in reproducing social inequalities.

6 Walford suggests the ideology of choice serves to mask the re-introduction of selective forms of education and to obscure the fact that failure in education stems from social disadvantage and poverty, not from making the wrong choices or being a bad parent. (1)

Wealth, Poverty and Welfare (pages 67–8 and 73)

Wealth and income

1 The two methods are the survey method (1) and the estates method. (1)

2 False. (1) Regressive taxes redistribute income and wealth from the poor to the rich.

3 Any two of the following: private pensions; medical insurance; education; mortgages; the NHS. (2)

4 Measurements based on household income don't take account of how income is distributed within the household. Women often get the smallest share. (1)

5 Two reasons suggested by Adonis and Pollard are: the growth of a new elite (1) and taxation policies. (1)

6 Davis and Moore believe income differences are necessary in order to attract the best people into the most important jobs. (1) This view is criticized by Marxists.

Poverty: definitions and measurement

1 Absolute poverty is defined in relation to subsistence as lacking the minimum needed for human survival. (1) Relative poverty is defined as being considerably below the average standard of living in a particular society. (1) The extent of relative poverty depends on the extent of inequality in a society.

2 The statement 'human needs are socially constructed' means that human needs are defined and created by society and so change over time and between societies. (1)

3 Mack and Lansley use a consensual definition based on public perceptions of poverty (1) and measure it using an index based on the items people consider essential. (1)

4 Any three of the following: women; ethnic minorities; pensioners; children; the unemployed; manual workers (especially unskilled); lone parents; the disabled. (3)

5 False. (1) 'Old' poverty (such as poverty amongst the elderly), has declined but 'new' poverty (such as unemployment) has increased.

Check yourself answers

Explanations of poverty

1 Lewis describes the culture of poverty as a distinctive sub-culture among the poor, with different values from mainstream society. (1) Coates and Silburn reject the idea because they found no evidence of it in their research. (1) Compare Lewis' explanation with Murray's.

2 *Murray* (1) uses the term underclass to describe a way of life which, he believes, has developed because of *over-generous welfare benefits*. (1) The availability of such benefits, he argues, encourages *unemployment* (1) amongst adults and *delinquency* (1) among the young.

3 **A** System-blaming. (1) The statement blames the economic system and not the poor themselves.

B Victim-blaming. (1) The statement points to poor people's lack of self-reliance as the cause. Marsland puts forward this type of explanation.

4 Dean and Taylor-Gooby describe claimants as 'reluctant dependents' because they wanted to work but were unable to find jobs. (1)

5 True. (1) Weber's concept of 'negatively privileged status group' helps to explain the poverty experienced by some ethnic minorities.

6 Women are over-represented amongst the poor because they are more likely than men to be in low-paid and/or part-time work, (1) lone parents, (1) and elderly. (1) Women are also less likely to receive an equal share of household income.

7 Poverty serves capitalism by: keeping wages down; (1) fear of poverty acts as a form of social control; (1) poverty divides the working class and discourages united action to change things. (1)

Welfare

1 For Beveridge the five giant evils were: want; idleness; squalor; disease; ignorance. (5)

2 False. (1) Means-tested benefits are targeted only at those who need them. Remember to contrast means-tested benefits with universal benefits.

3 **A** New Right. (1) This view stresses the need for families to be self-reliant and the role of the state reduced.

B Feminist. (1) The statement is one of the key criticisms feminists make of the welfare state. Concepts of patriarchy and dependency are central to feminist explanations of welfare.

C Social democratic. (1) The reference to equality through gradual reform tells us this is a social democratic perspective. This contrasts with the Marxist view that revolution not reform is the way to bring about social equality.

4 Welfare pluralism is where there are many different providers: public, private, voluntary and informal. (1)

5 Community care has been criticized as an excuse for cutting costs (1) and for shifting responsibility from the state to women in the family. (1)

6 The 'affordable welfare state' is a view that improvements in the welfare state have to be paid for by improved economic performance. (1)

Check yourself answers

WORK AND LEISURE (pages 80–1 and 86)

The management and control of work

1 False. (1) Weber believed bureaucracy was the most efficient type of organization.
2 Scientific management means the introduction of time and motion, (1) financial incentives (1) and the selection and training of workers (1) to improve industrial output and efficiency. (1)
3 Human Relations school criticizes Taylor for ignoring informal work groups. (1) Seen from a Marxist perspective, both Scientific Management and Human Relations are simply methods of extracting more profit from the workforce.
4 Mayo conducted research at the Hawthorne plant. (1)
5 Braverman argues that *deskilling* (1) results from *mass production* (1) because it reduces work to a series of unskilled tasks. More recently, research on the impact of *information technology* (1) has shown that its effects vary, causing *upskilling* (1) of some jobs and deskilling of others.
6 Any three of the following: compression of time and space; 24-hour world financial markets; multi-nationals dominating trade; global production methods; increased competition for global markets; spread of the Internet. (3)
7 Any two of the following differences: mass vs. specialized production; mass vs. niche markets; sharp division vs. integration of manual and mental work; centralized vs. delegated decision-making. (2) Fordism gets it name from the production methods used on the Ford assembly line.

Alienation and work satisfaction

1 The four dimensions are powerlessness; meaninglessness; isolation; self-estrangement. (4)
2 Blauner describes the relationship between alienation and technology by plotting an *inverted U curve* (1) on a graph. The graph shows that although alienation reaches a peak with *mass production*, (1) the introduction of *automation* (1) reduces alienation because workers are given more control of *decision-making*. (1)
3 Goldthorpe and Lockwood identify workers' orientations or attitudes to work as the key factor affecting work satisfaction. (1)
4 Gallie suggests French and British workers have different political cultures. (1) These findings lead to criticisms of Blauner's view that technology alone determines work satisfaction.
5 True. (1) Postmodernists argue that paid employment has declined in importance as a source of identity.

Check yourself answers

Conflict at work

1 **A** Marxist. (1) The reference to class exploitation indicates it is the Marxist perspective.

B Functionalist. (1) This explanation is based on the functionalist view that society is basically integrated and consensual, therefore conflict is due to 'breakdown'. In this view, strikes are a form of deviance.

2 Lane and Roberts described strikes as 'perfectly normal events'. (1)

3 Any three of the following reasons: legal/policy changes; rising unemployment; distancing of the unions by government; management of public opinion; privatization; controls on public sector pay; new technology; economic restructuring. (3)

4 Any four of the following: absenteeism; labour-turnover; intimidatory humour; cheating/pilfering; industrial sabotage; harassment. (4)

Unemployment

1 Social groups who may experience unemployment because of discrimination include women, ethnic minorities, older people, the disabled and school leavers. (4)

2 Three ways in which unemployment is defined are the headline figure (or claimant count), (1) the ILO definition (1) and the Unemployment Unit's definition. (1)

3 Examples are unpaid domestic work, moonlighting or the informal economy and criminal activities. (3) Some people are neither in work nor counted as unemployed, for example, those on government training schemes.

4 False. (1) Pahl found no evidence of role-reversal amongst couples where the husband was unemployed.

5 Allatt and Yeandle found that the young unemployed experienced loss of identity and self-esteem (sickness and depression), often withdrawing from their families. (1)

Leisure

1 **A** The opposition pattern. (1) It is characterized by a sharp distinction between work and leisure.

B The extension pattern. (1) It is characterized by a lack of separation between work and leisure. Remember Parker puts forward three leisure patterns, including the neutrality pattern.

2 Apart from work, Roberts identifies age, (1) gender, (1) family cycle (1) and individual choice (1) as shaping leisure patterns.

3 Any three of the following reasons: venues are often male-dominated; financial restrictions; lack of transport; fear of street crime; domestic responsibilities; cultural definitions of femininity. (3)

4 Clarke and Critcher approach the study of leisure historically by showing how the idea of *rational recreation* (1) became a way to control working class leisure in the 19th century, and how *consumer capitalism* (1) developed in the 20th century. Both these developments are examples of how the ruling class has maintained its *hegemony.* (1)

5 True. (1) Postmodernists believe that in today's society the choices people make about what to buy and consume greatly influence their identities. This view challenges Parker's view that occupation has a major influence on leisure patterns.
6 Scase believes occupation remains central to personal identity because position in the labour market determines access to resources and opportunities for leisure. (1)

SOCIOLOGICAL METHODS (pages 93 and 99–100)

Types and sources of data/Experiments

1 Three examples are questionnaires, structured interviews and official statistics. (3)
2 Primary data is collected 'first hand' by sociologists themselves for their own sociological purposes. (1) Secondary data is not collected by sociologists themselves. (1)
3 The seven criteria are validity, reliability, representativeness, practical considerations, subject matter, ethics and theoretical perspective. (7)
4 Experiments are seldom used because they create an artificial situation, (1) because of ethical reasons, (1) and because society is too large. (1) This is an important difference between sociology and natural sciences.

Survey methods

1 They provide a trial-run to identify problems to be ironed out before the main survey. (1)
2 Quota sampling is where a researcher has to find a set number of respondents who fit into social categories required by the survey, such as a certain number of men. (1) Quota samples are more widely used in market research than sociology.
3 Follow-up questionnaires and interviews reduce the rate of non-response. (1) The problem with non-response is that it is non-random.
4 All respondents answer the same questions (1) and respondents are not influenced by an interviewer being present. (1)
5 False. (1) Structured interviews do not give scope for a conversation to develop. The interviewer and interviewee are restricted to pre-set questions.
6 Any three of the following: non-response; people not completing all the questions; respondents can't express true feelings because questions are pre-coded; respondents may lie, forget things or exaggerate in their answers; they may misunderstand the question. (3)
7 Dean and Taylor-Gooby used semi-structured interviews. (1)
8 Unstructured interviews are criticized as unreliable because no two interviews are alike. (1)
9 False. (1) Unstructured interviews give more scope for empathy than structured interviews can.

Check yourself answers

10 Interviewer effect is where interviewees react differently depending on the type of interviewer, (1) for example, they may give different replies to male and female interviewers. (1)

Observational methods

1 Pryce allowed a hypothesis to emerge in his study 'Endless Pressure'. (1)
2 With covert PO researchers conceal their true identity and purpose, (1) but with overt observation they don't. (1)
3 Any two of the following: asking questions; taking notes (without others knowing); risk of cover being blown; risk of personal injury; arrest. (2)
4 Humphreys is criticized for disregarding ethics. (1) There are now ethical guidelines sociologists are expected to follow when doing research.
5 'Going native' means the observer becomes completely involved with the group and begins to see everything the way the group sees it. (1)
6 The stages of PO are getting in, staying in and getting out. (3)
7 The main advantage of PO is that it takes place in *natural settings* (1) which allows the researcher to get closer to the real lives of the people being observed. Supporters therefore claim that PO can produce *uniquely valid data*. (1) One of the main disadvantages of PO is that research is on a *small scale* (1), making it difficult to generalize about the findings. Critics argue that PO lacks *re-test reliability* (1) because similar studies carried out by other sociologists are unlikely to produce the same results.

Secondary sources

1 The two main methods used for collection of government statistics are registration (1) and surveys. (1)
2 **A** Marxist. (1) The reference to state manipulation of information suggests this is a Marxist view.
B Interactionist. (1) The reference to social construction points to an interactionist view. Interactionist studies of crime and suicide illustrate the social construction of official statistics.
C Positivist. (1) In this view, official statistics are a source of objective data.
3 False. (1) Newspapers are a source of secondary data.
4 Thomas and Znaniecki used letters, (1) biographies and autobiographies (1) and public documents (including newspaper articles, court and social work documents). (1)
5 An example of content analysis is 'Bad News' by the Glasgow University Media Group. (1) Studies of the mass media make extensive use of content analysis.

Case studies, longitudinal studies and triangulation

1 False. (1) Case studies focus on a particular case or example.
2 A longitudinal study follows a sample over a period of time. (1) Examples include Douglas' study (1) and the National Child Development Survey. (1)
3 False. (1) Triangulation sounds like it should be three, but in fact it means looking at something from more than one point of view.

Check yourself answers

THE INDIVIDUAL AND SOCIETY (page 106)

Culture and socialization

1 False. (1) Most social behaviour is learned.
2 Socialization is the learning (or internalization) of a culture. (1)
3 Culture is transmitted, (1) learned (1) and shared. (1)
4 False. (1) It is responsible for primary socialization whilst the school is the main agency of secondary socialization. Parsons uses the term secondary socialization to describe formal education.

Social structure

1 Social role refers to the set of norms that define the behaviour expected of a social actor. (1)
2 **A** True. (1) Interactionists criticize functionalism for putting forward an over-socialized view that fails to recognize that individuals have choice.
  B True. (1) Marxists criticize functionalism for putting forward an over-integrated view of society which ignores conflict and exploitation.
3 By 'taking' roles, Turner means that we learn to play the roles society gives us. (1) By 'making' roles he means that we create roles ourselves. (1) The distinction between taking and making social roles shows that society involves social structure and social action.

Identity

1 Identity refers to our sense of self, who we identify with, and who we think we are. (1) Identity is a key concept for postmodernists.
2 Class identity is about how a person sees their class position. Marx argued that the working class acquires *class consciousness* (1) when workers see themselves as part of the same class and unite to change society. However, Marx also describes how some workers suffer from *false consciousness* and do not recognize that their true enemy is the capitalist class. (1) An example of the latter is *racism* (1) which sets workers against each other.
3 Oakley describes sex as the biological differences between male and female, (1) whereas gender refers to psychological and cultural differences between men and women. (1) Consider the differences between sex, gender and sexuality.
4 Ethnicity refers to cultural heritage and identity, (1) whereas race refers to the supposed biological differences between 'races'. (1)
5 True. (1) National identity involves identifying with a nation or nation-state.
6 True. (1) Postmodernists and Marxists have different views about the importance of social class compared with other sources of social difference and inequality.

INDEX